Young
2004 POETRY C

ONCE UPON A RHYME

IMAGINATION FOR A NEW GENERATION

Northern Counties
Edited by Steve Twelvetree

Young**Writers**

First published in Great Britain in 2004 by:
Young Writers
Remus House
Coltsfoot Drive
Peterborough
PE2 9JX
Telephone: 01733 890066
Website: www.youngwriters.co.uk

SB ISBN 1 84460 579 5

Foreword

Young Writers was established in 1991 and has been passionately devoted to the promotion of reading and writing in children and young adults ever since. The quest continues today. Young Writers remains as committed to engendering the fostering of burgeoning poetic and literary talent as ever.

This year's Young Writers competition has proven as vibrant and dynamic as ever and we are delighted to present a showcase of the best poetry from across the UK. Each poem has been carefully selected from a wealth of *Once Upon A Rhyme* entries before ultimately being published in this, our twelfth primary school poetry series.

Once again, we have been supremely impressed by the overall high quality of the entries we have received. The imagination, energy and creativity which has gone into each young writer's entry made choosing the best poems a challenging and often difficult but ultimately hugely rewarding task - the general high standard of the work submitted amply vindicating this opportunity to bring their poetry to a larger appreciative audience.

We sincerely hope you are pleased with our final selection and that you will enjoy *Once Upon A Rhyme Northern Counties* for many years to come.

Contents

Chloe McMorris (11)	18
Elizabeth Walker (11)	18
James Musgrove (11)	18
Emma Flint (9)	19
Laura Jones (10)	19
Emma Hoey (10)	19
Jennifer Newcombe (11)	20
Nicole Alderson (11)	20
Danielle Shaw (9)	20
Conall Sweeting (9)	21
Jordan White (11)	21
Abigail Cawley (8)	21
Adele Harrison (9)	22
Jamie Montgomery (9)	22
Faye Donnison (8)	22
Jack Crute (8)	23
Tia Newton (9)	23
Arron Lyth (11)	23
Gabrielle Lincoln (10)	24
Jennifer Currell (8)	24
Nathan Dawson (8)	24
Danielle Potts (9)	25
Jessica Jordan (8)	25
Kirby Weegram (9)	25
Eden Bruce (9)	26
Laura Brallisford (11)	26
Daniel Bell (11)	26
Jessica Playfor (8)	27
Lloyd Tindall (9)	27
Matthew Henry (9)	28

Kader Primary School, Middlesbrough

Madeleine Clark (8)	28
Robert Scott (9)	28
Victoria French (9)	29
Rob Turley (8)	29
Jack Price (9)	29
Vidya Gosain (7)	30
Rebecca Chalk (8)	30
Emily Holden (8)	30

Lingfield Primary School, Middlesbrough

Rebecca Briggs (8)	31
Sam Bytheway (9)	31
Robyn Bulpitt (9)	32
Joshua Fox (9)	32
Andrew Busby (9)	33
Max Tweddle ((8)	33
Ellena Craggy (9)	34
Callum Woodhouse (10)	34
Adam Davies (9)	35
Mathew Pearson (9)	35
Tabby Hicks (9)	36
Lucy Taylor (9)	36
Isabel Humphreys (9)	37
Jessica Edwards (10)	37
Jack Hunter (9)	38
Robert Kerr (9)	38
Sally Ivison (9)	39
Alice Blott (10)	39
Mina Jackson (9)	40
Alex Dampier (10)	40
Andrew Harland (9)	41
Matthew Clarke (10)	41
Abbie McDonald (9)	42
Jessica Watts (10)	42
Alan Milburn (9)	43
Jade Burton (10)	43
Megan Iley (10)	44
Alice Smith (10)	44
Georgina Nicholls (8)	45
Conor Spencer (9)	45
Sam Pearson (9)	46
Stephanie Barker (10)	46
Matthew Emery (10)	47
Laura Readman (8)	47
Alex Hatfield (9)	48
Chloe Whitby (8)	48
Claire Everitt (9)	49
Isabel Carruthers (8)	49
Alexandra Walker (8)	50
Kieran Woodhouse (10)	50

Dale Scurr (10)	50
Olivia Thompson (8)	51
Dale Readman (10)	51
Jordan Spencer (9)	51
Benjamin Learwood (8)	52
Sam Peirson (8)	52
Elliot Duffy (8)	52
Thomas Matthews (8)	53
Katie Parkes (8)	53
John Phellas (8)	53
Eve Craggy (8)	54
Jade Taylor (8)	54
Jenny Craggy (10)	54

Northgate Junior School, Guisborough

Rachel Sykes (11)	55
James Bowes (11)	55
Natasha Dickinson (10)	56
Sophie Crawford (10)	56
Eleanor Matthews (9)	57
James Mayhew (11)	57
Jade Clements (11)	58
Aimee Bruerton (11)	58
Lauren Smith (10)	58
Carl Reid (11)	59
Dane Matthewman (11)	59
Stacy Williams (11)	59
Simone Wye (10)	60
Lewis Johnson (11)	60
Eleanor Hewson (11)	60
Rachel Wallace (11)	61
Chelsee Breeze (11)	61
Chelsea Skidmore (11)	61
Jordan Corner (9)	62
Tyler Wedgwood (11)	62
Lucy Storey (11)	62
Jessica Williams (10)	63
Clare Peacock (9)	63
Sam Thompson (11)	63

Pallister Park Primary School, Middlesbrough

Ashley Fairburn (10)	64
Gabrielle Sadler-Hunt (9)	64
Bethany Williamson (10)	65
Jack Banks (10)	65
Ryan Jones (7)	65
Chloe McElwee (10)	66
Tasmin Bowes-Chester (10)	66
Cameron Corner (7)	66
Adam Pirie (9)	67
Leah McClelland (9)	67
Gemma Parkin (8)	67
Lloyd Evans (9)	68
Corrinna Richards (10)	68
Chelsea Smyth (7)	68
Abigail Davies (7)	69
Curtis Robinson (7)	69
Abbie Morris (7)	69
Ashleigh Ingledew (10)	70
Lindsey McClelland (9)	70
Amy Matthews (10)	71
Chantelle Smyth (9)	71
Bethany Cronin (9)	72
Nicole Llewellyn (8)	72
Jennifer Thomas (9)	73
Georgia Smith (8)	73
Beth Byrne (9)	74
Lyndsey Coleman (9)	74

Red Rose Primary School, Chester-Le-Street

Rachael Turnbull (9)	74
Holly Gardner (10)	75
Sarah Whitehouse (10)	76
Sarah Jones (10)	76
Abbie Davis (9)	77
Philippa Attle (10)	77
Megan Gardner (10)	78
Paul Roll (10)	79
Katie Miller (10)	80
Adam Clarke (10)	81
Ryan Curry (9)	82

Lauren Wilson (10)	83
Caroline Ray (9)	84
Emily Thompson (9)	85
Elizabeth Ray (9)	86
Kurt Dickinson (10)	87
Robert Jopling (10)	87
James Armstrong (10)	88

St Pius X Primary School, Middlesbrough

Joshua Allan (11)	88
Shanaz O'Brien (11)	89
Daisy Watkins (11)	89
Alex McLoughlin (11)	90
Louise Johnston (11)	90
Victoria Young (9)	91
Faye Humphreys (11)	91
Katie Vallely (10)	92
Jessica Connorton (11)	92
Lewis Armes (11)	93
Charlotte Mett (9)	93
Daniel March (10)	94
Ross McMenamin (10)	94
Michael Shaw (11)	95
Stephen Woodman (10)	95
Jack Davies (10)	96
Jack Bezance (9)	96
Katie Wilson (10)	97
Nathan Newman (10)	98
Aidan Chester (9)	98
Bethany James (9)	99
Chloe Welsh (10)	99
Sarah Walker (10)	100
Louise Walker (11)	100
Connor Ovington (10)	100
James Marsh (10)	101
Chloe Jones (10)	101
Ryan Chilver (8)	101
Hayley Pink (9)	102
Kyle McNamara (9)	102
Stephenie Roberts (8)	102
Jonathon Roche (8)	103

Aaron Webber (9)	103
Bradley Goulding (9)	103
Jessica Waite (8)	104
Ellie Leopard (8)	104
Andrew McElwee (9)	104
Carl Alexander (8)	105
Isabella Angioy (9)	105
Olivia Hopkin (8)	105

Shotton Hall Junior School, Peterlee

Sarah Dixon (10)	106
Laura Weatherall (11)	107
Adam Martin (11)	108
Kirsty Fishwick (10)	108
Mark Gibson (11)	109
Megan Thornley (8)	109
Kirsty Anne Farn (10)	110
Michael Newhouse (11)	110
Liam Goodfellow (9)	111
Nicholas Turnbull (10)	111
Joanne Holborg (10)	112
Alex Gibson (10)	112
Samantha Hepworth (11)	113
Lauren Bannister (10)	113
Tasmin Duggan (11)	113
Sarah French (10)	114
Tim Evans (11)	114
Annie Harris (9)	115
Vicky Bentham (10)	115
Michelle Burey (11)	115
Paige McGoldrick (9)	116
Jack Anderson (9)	116

Skerne Park Primary School, Darlington

Victoria Dennis (8)	116
Terri Stephens (11)	117
Shivaun Barnes (10)	117
Ashley Pascoe (11)	118
Lily McGonigal (8)	118
Annabel Townsend (11)	119
Lauren Mitchinson (11)	119

Jordan Bateman (8)	120
Stacy Knight (8)	120
Kayleigh Reddington (8)	121
Caitlin Longstaff (11)	121
Luci Purves (8)	121
Andrew Colley (8)	122
Paige Cooper (9)	122
Elijah Taylor (10)	122
Zoe Hunter (11)	123
Victoria Butcher (11)	123
Christopher House (11)	123
Amanda Fitzpatrick (10)	124
Ryan Burton (8)	124
Christopher Hull (10)	124
Autumn Robson (11)	125
Rebecca Stirland (11)	125
Sarah Dunn (9)	126
Rachel Curle (10)	126

Viewley Hill Primary School, Middlesbrough

David Bigham (8)	126
Gabrielle Leighton (8)	127
Kierra Sargent (8)	127
Bradley Wilkinson (8)	127
Lewis Danks (9)	128
Ashley Charlton (9)	128
Mikki-Jo Blades (9)	129
Matthew Kay (9)	129
Ryan Phillips (9)	130
Katie Taylor (8)	130
John-Paul Stone (9)	130
Rachael Miller (9)	131
Billy Horrigan (9)	131
Samantha Lappin (9)	131
Jay Morrison (9)	132
Amber Daly (9)	132

Village Primary School, Thornaby

Anthony Kippax (10)	132
Arron Butta (11)	133
Vanessa Butterworth (11)	133

The Poems

Seasons

Lambs dance and prance around,
While chicks lay with their mother
Feeling safe and sound
Chicks' fluffy fur and lambs woolly coat.
All signs that spring has approached.

Children playing, laughter heard
A chorus from a single bird
Flowers blooming in the sun
This is summer it's begun.

Rain falls from the sky
Because it's cooler, that's why
But still everyone can have some fun
As autumn has barely begun.

Snowflakes are icy cold
Warm fires look like gold
As the snowdrops fall around
They silently touch the ground
It is winter, enjoy the snow,
As spring is not far to go.

Faye Richardson (11)
Fens Primary School, Hartlepool

The Sea

The sea lashed and crashed on the shore,
And gave a mighty and ferocious roar.

Small fishing boats and ships sailed along,
With their crew singing a pirate song.

But when the ocean is rather quite calm,
It cannot really do much harm.

In the hot, summer sun when children play,
The ocean has only a gentle sway.

Amy Bowman (10)
Fens Primary School, Hartlepool

My Dad's Car

My dad's car
Sticks to the road like tar.
The car is like a slug,
It might be quicker to catch a bug.
The colours are really bright,
They will dazzle your sight.
No wonder,
He polishes it every Sunday.
When summer comes,
And we go to the beach,
We get in the car, it smells like bleach.
If we get sand in there,
He will lose all his hair.
Then one day it was stolen
By Mr Lolen.
He sold it bit by bit,
And then that was the end of it.

Craig Priestman (11)
Fens Primary School, Hartlepool

Summertime

I love summertime,
Children skipping to their favourite rhyme,
The way the sun rays fall on my face,
And children running around full of grace.

Having days at the beach,
Watching the sea go out beyond your reach,
Miles of golden sand,
And fish and chip shops all at hand.

Parks full of flowers,
Children and adults having picnics for hours,
Relaxing in the sun
Having so much fun.

Rachel Carroll (11)
Fens Primary School, Hartlepool

Cinderella

Wanted, the lovely lady
That fits the glass slipper,
She's my little star
She shimmers and glitters,
In the moonlight sky

If I find my fair lady
She will be wed to me,
Her head will be fitted into a crown,
She will wear a gorgeous wedding gown

Oh, lovely lady come to me
If you do I'll dance with glee,
Be mine, be mine, oh lady come
For we will drink lots of rum

Now if this poem has not caught your eye
Then oh my darling, I say goodbye,
But please come and be married to me,
You only have 'til ten past three

The wedding is booked
Oh my darling beauty,
There will be no finer
Couple than you and me
So come my lady and marry me!

Kim Barker-Platt (10)
Fens Primary School, Hartlepool

Stars

Star bright, star light
Stars shining in the night
That's the time to go to sleep
So I count my blessing instead of sheep.

Emma Woolston (7)
Fens Primary School, Hartlepool

Pet Day

It was pet day at school today
Fiona brought her frog
After a bit of delay
David brought his dog
Gemma brought her guinea pig
Simon brought his snake
Tommy brought his tortoise
It wasn't even awake.
The teacher said 'Very good class
You've done really, really well.'
I looked up at the clock and I
Heard the home-time bell.
When I got home from school today
I gave my mum a shock
Because in my school bag I had
Brought back a dog, a guinea
Pig, a snake and a tortoise
That still wasn't awake.
And not forgetting the school clock!

Louanne Astley (8)
Fens Primary School, Hartlepool

An Advertisement

Have you seen seven dwarves?
With trousers the colour of mauve,
Even some with beards perhaps
And some with pointy sleeping caps,
If you do please reply,
By the 5th of July
The address is,
55 summer whizz.

Rachel Wheelhouse (11)
Fens Primary School, Hartlepool

Dogs

Spotty dogs,
Black and white,
Patches here,
Patches there,
Patches everywhere.

Dogs bark,
Dogs sing,
Dogs howl,
Dogs everywhere.

Big dogs,
Small dogs,
Fat and thin,
Different dogs everywhere.

Eating bones,
Wagging tails,
Smooth coats,
Howling at their owner.

Olivia Proudlock (9)
Fens Primary School, Hartlepool

Water

Water, water,
So much fun!
Water, water,
Everyone!

Water, water
Take a drink!
Water, water
Don't stare or blink!

Water, water
So fresh and clear!
Water, water
No fear!

Jacob Wright (7)
Fens Primary School, Hartlepool

My Dog

I have a dog named Lucy
She is brown and likes to eat
She wiggles her tail and booty
Whenever she comes to greet

I have a dog named Lucy
She barks at me a lot
I give her dinner and water
And often a treat of chocs

I have a dog named Lucy
I love her ever so much
At night she sleeps on my bed
She snores and keeps me up

I have a dog named Lucy
She's all grown up now
Her tail is short and stumpy
But she's one of the family anyhow.

Jordan Feeney (9)
Fens Primary School, Hartlepool

My Guinea Pig

Georgina is my pet,
I love her very much.
She is a guinea pig and lives in a hutch,
When she's in the sort of mood
She will eat any food.
We put her in the garden
To go and nibble grass
She has a special house,
With a hole cut in
Just like a mouse!
Every night when I go to bed
I go to her cage and peek
And in return she says 'Squeak! Squeak!'

Rebecca Walker (9)
Fens Primary School, Hartlepool

One School Day

Every morning at five minutes to nine
Into school I go feeling fine
Registration, English then maths,
Then playtime where I have a few laughs
Back into class for some history
Learning about Cook sailing the sea.

Lunchtime, oh the food is great
Eat everything that's put on my plate
Off to play with all of my friends
The bells ring when lunchtime ends
Straight into class, get changed for PE
Trip playing football, fell and hurt my knee.

Get back into class, quick change then sit
Teacher tells us off about our PE kit
Music starts we're making a song
Our group's lyrics start to go wrong
Teacher shouts, 'Now it's tidy up time'
I go out of school feeling fine.

Liam Wild (11)
Fens Primary School, Hartlepool

Help The Harp

As I always fall,
I need someone very tall,
Can you climb?
If you can, there's more than one vine,
Come and find the golden harp,
It's not like catching any carp,
Climb the beanstalk,
Do not walk,
Come on, run, or the job will be taken,
Get over here or the giant shall awaken,
Dare you enter the giant's castle?
Come on now, do not hassle!

Matthew Davies (10)
Fens Primary School, Hartlepool

The End Of The Day

The flaring sun lowers in the sky,
Lengthening the shadows of men,
Each day ends with a sunset,
And starts again with a sunrise.

Memorable things occur in the day,
Things you can remember for life,
But the most memorable thing, I think,
Is thinking of putting an end to strife.

The best time for this is the end of the day,
But you don't have to do the things that I say.

James Pattison (11)
Fens Primary School, Hartlepool

The Tiger

A flame of orangey-red,
A staring and growling head,
Slashes of white paint,
A set of whiskers so faint,
As it prowls through the jungle trees
Not a sound to be heard but the breeze.

Kristy Weegram (10)
Fens Primary School, Hartlepool

Ryan Goes Flying

There is a boy called Ryan
Whose dream was to go flying
He had a go
And broke his toe
And can't stop crying!

Jack Musgrave (10)
Fens Primary School, Hartlepool

What's War?

What's war when,
People fight, when,
Guns go bang and bullets shoot,
No noise is heard, no owls hoot.

Lord don't let war happen,
We pray let the people live,
Make the world live happily,
Alone with peace.

Laura Brooks (8)
Fens Primary School, Hartlepool

A Drunken Deer

When I saw a deer,
I think it had a beer,
And that's my fear,
So it came near.

When it was drunk,
It died on a tree trunk,
And killed a Japanese monk,
Which flattened a skunk!

Sam Tindall (10)
Fens Primary School, Hartlepool

My Pet

Holly's jolly,
She brushes herself on a mat
Holly's a bit of a wally,
She's definitely a mad cat
Holly has a dolly it looks a bit like a rat,
She smells like our parrot Polly
Just fancy that!

Melissa Sert (9)
Fens Primary School, Hartlepool

The Seasons

It's springtime and the flowers are peeping out
Blustery but sunny weather, people on country walks.
Everyone's excited with Easter on the way,
But spring isn't here to stay.

It's summer and out come the deckchairs,
Hot and sunny weather, cold drinks in the sun.
Everyone's excited with the holidays on the way,
But summer isn't here to stay.

It's autumn and brown leaves are tumbling down
Drizzly and windy weather and the warm thick clothes
                                    come out again
Everyone's excited with fireworks and Hallowe'en looking
                                    round the corner,
But autumn isn't here to stay.

It's winter and incredibly white snow covers the land
                                    sending it to rest
Cold and wet, woolly jumpers on but still having fun
Everyone's very excited with Christmas on the way
But winter isn't here to stay.

Claire Richardson (11)
Fens Primary School, Hartlepool

Mr Wolf

Send those thin piggies to me
And I'll fatten them up, you'll see
American, English I don't care
I'll even buy them tickets for the fair
A week or two at Butchershop House
And they'll no longer look like a mouse
They might take a while but don't worry
So don't be coming back in a hurry
Black, pink or any other colour
They'll be chubby so don't delay
Send them to Butchershop House.

Mohib Ellahi (11)
Fens Primary School, Hartlepool

The Fruit Bowl And The Football Match

I'm a nice round fruit bowl
With apples just lying there
And many other fruits
Waiting to be eaten
Before Chelsea are beaten

The apple is desperate to get out
So listen to the story of the apples

Seventy-six minutes are left of the football match
The fruit is lying there on the kitchen table
Waiting to be eaten

The living room cheers at half time
The family comes out of the living room
To have a tasty snack
So along comes Joe
Looking at the fruit bowl
Looking at the grapes, he takes them in a flash
Then comes Liam who takes the apples out
'Phew' said the apple right before Chelsea are beaten.

Liam Hedley (9)
Fens Primary School, Hartlepool

Handsome Prince

Cinderella needs a prince,
Her other boy smelled of mince,
He can't be fat, can't be thin,
Otherwise he will be in the bin.

Cinder likes boys who chatter,
If not it doesn't matter,
She's twenty-four,
So give her a go,
You won't regret, if you place this bet.

Danielle Steele (10)
Fens Primary School, Hartlepool

Poor Johnny

Poor Johnny hurt his arm
Sneaking into Mr Brown's farm.
He went in to steal a cow
How he would carry it I don't know how.

He thought his mother would like some beef,
Because she can't eat much with her false teeth,
With lots of veg and Yorkshire pud,
Thinking of others just like you should.

He climbed in through a broken gate,
To meet Paul, his very best mate.
As he dragged his leg through a hole
He caught his arm on a very sharp pole.

The blood was vast and very red
'You must go home' his best friend said
So off he went in lots of pain,
And I don't think he'll do that again!

Christopher Hodgson (11)
Fens Primary School, Hartlepool

Watch Out!

I found a little kangaroo
I named it little Jack
I asked if I could keep it
In the garden out the back

Mum said 'It will grow too big'
Dad said 'It'll be just fine'
So I kept the little kangaroo
Which grew and grew with time

It grew so big it had to go
Mum said 'I told you so'
Dad said 'I had my doubts'
So if you see my kangaroo
Watch out!

Lucy Pollin (9)
Fens Primary School, Hartlepool

Schooldays

Doors open, school has started,
All troublemakers have been parted.
Lessons are soon beginning,
Soon it will be assembly time
And children will be singing.

The bell rings, it is dinner time,
Hungry children make a line.
Lessons soon start,
Children working hard to do their part.

The bell rings, time to go home,
Children walk home but not alone.
Teachers plan for the next day,
While children go home and play.

Soon it is time for teachers to go home,
And this is the end to my poem.

Rebecca Cawley (11)
Fens Primary School, Hartlepool

A Fish Goes . . .

A fish goes . . .
Bubble, bubble, bubble
Swim, swim, swim
Breathe, breathe, breathe
All day long.

There are different kinds of fish
In different countries
They are coming in different shapes
And colours too.

Some are fierce or even frightening
But watch out because I am going to get you
Snap, snap.

Tamsin Williamson (8)
Fens Primary School, Hartlepool

Dancing Dork

The school disco happens once every year
And the dork of the school happened to wear,
A black bin liner held up by a clip
And slapped on her face was bright pink lipstick
In her old battered shoes she stumbled to
The open doors, which she quickly went through
Her strange dance moves made everybody stare
The children were shocked that she did not care
Each window was broken from her screeching voice
And the children felt that they had no choice
So away from the school building they ran
Sprinting home, in a car, or in their van.
They left the dancing dork all alone
Till 9:00pm she was on her own
In the morning came a normal school day
The dork herself again, with friend Faye.
The two girls are known as dorks of the school
Geeky and freaky they could never be cool.

Jane Robson (11)
Fens Primary School, Hartlepool

The Wedding Day

Today Miss Brown would become a Mrs,
She was so nervous she had the jitters,
Her husband to be was in such a rush,
He was so late he fell in a bush,
When he finally got into the church,
He changed his mind, turned and forward he lurched,
Right into the aunties and granny
Whose fashion was pretty uncanny
The wedding was such a sight,
It was almost night,
She flung him on the floor,
And tossed him out the door.

Natasha Edmanson (11)
Fens Primary School, Hartlepool

Young Mr You-Know-Who

Young Mr You-Know-Who
He needed the loo,
He climbed up the watch-ma-call-it,
To do what he needed to do,
He opened the door,
Feeling he needed it more,
Hearing a crack,
Then suddenly falling through the floor.

Young Mr You-Know-Who,
Whatever should he do?
He shouted, 'Oh dear,
Now I really need the loo'
He ran up the thing-a-ma-bob,
Staring at the door
Reaching out to open it and hoping not to fall through the floor.

Young Mr You-Know-Who,
Who finished from the loo,
He opened the door,
Suddenly falling to the next floor,
He stood up with dust on his face,
Looking at his untied lace,
Young Mr You-Know-Who who then thought,
Deciding he needed the loo some more.

Anthony Davison (11)
Fens Primary School, Hartlepool

Laura

There once was a girl called Laura,
Whose nickname was always Nora.
She ate tons of sweets,
Took up ten seats
And now she always wears
Diadora.

Sean Sweeney (11)
Fens Primary School, Hartlepool

The Giant

Come to me
I would like a bee
I'm big and thick
Come and chop this stick

I forget my name
I play games
The stick is green
It's made of beans
Reply to www.biggiant.com.

Jonathan Grundy (10)
Fens Primary School, Hartlepool

Gardens

Is your garden the worst of all?
If it is come and have a ball
Pick up the phone and ring the garden man
And he will be around in his big white van.

He will make your garden right,
He will also make your grass so bright
Even though it is as dark as the night.

Lewis Dunnett (10)
Fens Primary School, Hartlepool

There Was An Old Man

There was an old man called Fred
Who always thought he was dead
Then one day
He could not pay
And there goes his scruffy old bed.

Thomas Rudd (10)
Fens Primary School, Hartlepool

Memories Of My First Dog

I remember when I was three
Seeing Snoopy for the first time
Just a cute little puppy
Exploring my skin with his tongue.

Jumping around as happy can be
Looking at me with those
Cute brown eyes
Full of wonder
Full of excitement
I started stroking him gently.

Jessica Maddison (10)
Fens Primary School, Hartlepool

Wind

The wind is like a bully,
Pushing over the weak people
And pestering the strong.

On a good day, the wind is peaceful
Yet on a bad day,
The wind is a terrifying storm.

People like the wind on a good day
So they can relax and be happy.

Katie McLaren (11)
Fens Primary School, Hartlepool

Stan

There was a young man called Stan
Who bought a second-hand van.
He took it to Spain
It did nothing but rain
So he didn't come home with a tan.

Jordan Cranney (11)
Fens Primary School, Hartlepool

My Aunt Mary

When I visited my aunt Mary,
From a distance she looked quite scary.
Her face was spotty and her nose was big,
On her head she was wearing a long wig.
She looked very old and acted like a hippy,
Right around her mouth was smudged orange lippy.

But when I got up close, I realised I was wrong,
It wasn't my aunt but my mum singing a song.
My cheeks turned scarlet and I fell on the floor,
I told her, 'Shut up, I can take it no more!'

Chloe McMorris (11)
Fens Primary School, Hartlepool

Little Miss Pretty Face

Little Miss Pretty Face, Charlotte Simpson,
Went to her school with a very tight bun.
The bun was so tight it tugged at her hair,
The bobble was nice but people did stare.
She walked into school feeling quite dizzy,
Everyone laughed except her friend Lizzie.
'Are you alright? You are looking unwell.'
And with that to the classroom floor she fell!

Elizabeth Walker (11)
Fens Primary School, Hartlepool

Betty

There was an old lady called Betty
Who ate a lot of spaghetti
She went to the Alps
Scratched some scalps
And then was ate by a yeti.

James Musgrove (11)
Fens Primary School, Hartlepool

The Furry Riddle

Man's best friend
Padding softly between strange
Obstacles

Furry playmate
Hopeful eyed
Tongue-lolling, mouth-slobbering

Wet-nosed
Sound of a tree
My playing never-ending.

Emma Flint (9)
Fens Primary School, Hartlepool

Me And My Friends

Me and my friends
We never fight
We never kick and punch
Best friends for ever and ever
We're just like sisters
We'll never split
We'll be together forever.
Friends 'til the end.

Laura Jones (10)
Fens Primary School, Hartlepool

What I Would Like!

I really would like a cat,
Not a dog or a rat,
I don't want a squawking parrot
Or a bunny with a carrot,
I wouldn't want a squeaking bat,
I'd prefer a tabby cat.

Emma Hoey (10)
Fens Primary School, Hartlepool

Me And My Dog

Happy memories, me and my dog shared
Like when I was three,
As I was running around with my cheeky grin
Saying 'Catch me, catch me if you can.'
Running as fast as I could
With my little legs circling up and down
Suddenly my happiness stopped
My heart broke
Tears rolled down my cheeks
People think that I have got over it
But I haven't
Deep down inside
At least my dog has gone to a happy place.

Jennifer Newcombe (11)
Fens Primary School, Hartlepool

I Have A Good Friend Called Lizzy

I have a good friend called Lizzy
Who loves to eat sweets that are fizzy
They make her feel ill
So she took an enormous pill
And now she's extremely dizzy.

Nicole Alderson (11)
Fens Primary School, Hartlepool

Jasmine The Juggler

Jasmine the Japanese juggler, juggled jelly in July.
Jasmine the Japanese juggler, juggled jelly while jumping high!
Jasmine the Japanese juggler, married a man from Timbuktu.
His name was Jim, and he could juggle too.

Danielle Shaw (9)
Fens Primary School, Hartlepool

Hard Work

Sweat dripping off your face,
Face red as a shy little baby,
Huge bangs like the loudest noise you have every heard
Pain eking through your veins and bones
Back wet as a swimming pool.
Eyes half closed of long time hours
Blood coming from all parts of your body
You need to be a strong man
Fast and good with weapons
And you can live with no food and water for a couple of days
The work I was thinking of
Was the army when all your teammates are dead
You're the last one.

Conall Sweeting (9)
Fens Primary School, Hartlepool

Everything Nice

The other day I lobbed the ball,
Right over a ten foot wall,
It hit a person on the head,
I didn't know if he was alive or dead.
On the fourth of July,
I squashed a fly,
I heard it scream and moan and cry,
Everybody knows how they have to die.

Jordan White (11)
Fens Primary School, Hartlepool

Fat Ellie

Ellie with the fat belly came in to watch telly with me and Kelly
We all sat down and span around and ate jam and jelly
Ellie and Kelly made the jelly and I made the jam and some ham
It was yummy.

Abigail Cawley (8)
Fens Primary School, Hartlepool

The Black Furry Riddle

Night walker
Ground digger
Worm eater
Den underground
Kill mice
Pink nose
Great sniffer
Black fur
Are so blind
Ball roller
Water drinker
Tunnel maker
Ground scratcher.

Adele Harrison (9)
Fens Primary School, Hartlepool

Wild Thing

Hinged back,
Human killer,
Smashing tail,
Boat sinker,
Meat-eating carnivore.

Jamie Montgomery (9)
Fens Primary School, Hartlepool

Birds

Birds are wonderful as can be,
Singing beautifully as you can see
Beautiful singing, ringing in my ears,
I wish I was a bird with healing tears.

Faye Donnison (8)
Fens Primary School, Hartlepool

The Spiked Riddle

Spiked bowling ball
Rolling to the skittles
Wet nosed, needled back

Slow eater,
Night prowler
Quiet as
Night

Dog's dinner stealer
Really sneaky hider
Curling up in a ball
My spiky full stop.

Jack Crute (8)
Fens Primary School, Hartlepool

Kangaroo, Kangaroo

Kangaroo, kangaroo
Jumping high and low.
To see the sight it is so fun,
But now it's time to go.

Kangaroo, kangaroo
Bouncing low and high.
Now it is time, we have to leave,
Goodbye, goodbye, goodbye.

Tia Newton (9)
Fens Primary School, Hartlepool

Tom

There once was a boy called Tom
Who went to scream at his mom
His mom gave him a clip
And also some lip
Then he was exploded by a bomb.

Arron Lyth (11)
Fens Primary School, Hartlepool

Burning Hands

I remember touching the scorching glass,
Burning my tender hands
I thought the fire behind the glass was attractive.
There were colours like red, gold, orange and yellow,
My hands were terribly blood-red
I screamed with pain
Mummy rushed frantically into the living room,
She thrust my hands into icy cold water
My hands turned cool but I remember the soreness most.

Gabrielle Lincoln (10)
Fens Primary School, Hartlepool

Snake

Slimy backed
Shivering shaker, sliding hissing
Spiked fangs
Shooting tongue
Wriggling body
Poison
Death slitherer, slider
Scaly backed
Quiet in wait lying.

Jennifer Currell (8)
Fens Primary School, Hartlepool

The Gunner

Donut eater,
Coffee drinker
Small thumbed
Tall gunned
Cool dude,
Small mude.

Nathan Dawson (8)
Fens Primary School, Hartlepool

Hedgehog

Rolling ball,
Spiky back,
Insect eater,
Slow crawler,
Pinned back.
Long-nosed,
Black eyed,
Night walker,
Shy stroller.
Leafed pin cushion
Snail-trailer.

Danielle Potts (9)
Fens Primary School, Hartlepool

Fur Ball

I have something fluffy
It thinks it's so, so funny
It leaps all day and plays and plays
To keep the cats away.

I have a fur ball somewhere on my body
My ear got so tired, so tired
And they flap from side to side.

Jessica Jordan (8)
Fens Primary School, Hartlepool

Who Am I?

Its tail swings from side to side.
Its whiskers twitch all the time.
Its kittens away asleep in bed.
Tabby, tabby, tabby
Do you know what I am?

Kirby Weegram (9)
Fens Primary School, Hartlepool

A Big Grey Riddle

Jungle living
Leaf eating
Floor shaking
Water blowing
Ear flapping
Grey giant
Heavy body
Tree trunk legs
Sharp tusks
Gentle nature.

Eden Bruce (9)
Fens Primary School, Hartlepool

School Dinners

Lining in the dinner hallee
Waiting for some greasy roastees
For desert some wobbly jellee
Shaped like an old man's bellee
And last of all some orange juicee
Looking for the perfect seatee

Sitting in the diner hallee
Eating my delicious lunchee
Oh how I am enjoying my lunch so much!

Laura Brallisford (11)
Fens Primary School, Hartlepool

The Dot Or Spot

There was an old lady called Dot
Who had the world's biggest spot,
Did she have a plan to destroy the spot?
Probably not,
The poor old lady called Dot who had the world's biggest spot
Did nothing.

Daniel Bell (11)
Fens Primary School, Hartlepool

Friends

I've got a friend
Well I think she's my friend
Because my friend who I think she's my friend
Might not be my friend
But I'm still her friend
Even though she might not be my friend
But it's alright now because I know she
Is not my friend
So I don't have to worry now
Because I know she is not my friend
So there is nothing to worry about
Because she is not my friend
And now I'm not her friend.

Jessica Playfor (8)
Fens Primary School, Hartlepool

What Do Crocodiles Do?

Armoured back,
Spiked arms
Swirling through dark water.

Warriors headpiece long snout
Vesseled blood, multi eye
Underwater predator.

Pale skin
Double teeth
Rolling eyeball
Lethal tail.

Lloyd Tindall (9)
Fens Primary School, Hartlepool

The Man's Best Friend

Man's best friend
Furry face and
Salivary chops
Intimidated heart
Excited life
Diving through the grass
Vampire-like teeth
Clawing through the plants
Exploring from place to place.

Matthew Henry (9)
Fens Primary School, Hartlepool

Knowbreak Castle

In Knowbreak Castle the wind blows and blows,
In Knowbreak Castle the sea flows and flows.
In Knowbreak Castle up the stairs you creep,
In Knowbreak Castle you hear a loud creak
In Knowbreak Castle you're in the dark,
In Knowbreak Castle there comes a big spark
In Knowbreak Castle things start to move,
In Knowbreak Castle they start to groove,
Then I run out of the doom and faint on the floor.

Madeleine Clark (8)
Kader Primary School, Middlesbrough

Name Poem

R abbits grazing on the grass,
O tters swimming in the stream,
B lue tits fluttering and flying,
E arwigs chewing on some cheese,
R ottweillers chomping on some rats,
T igers messing with some meat.

Robert Scott (9)
Kader Primary School, Middlesbrough

In The Dark Of Night

In the dark of the night when all is still
Down my back I feel a chill
The hoot of the owl and the purr of the cat
The branch on my window goes rat-a-tat-tat.

In the dark of night in the land of dreams
Nothing is quite how it seems
Monsters and witches come out and play
They stay out until the light of day.

In the dark of night while we sleep
Ghosts and ghouls come out and creep
They dance and play all night long
And in the morning they go back where they belong.

Victoria French (9)
Kader Primary School, Middlesbrough

The Roman And The Celt

Once upon a rhyme,
A Roman soldier said 'What's the time?'
A Celtic warrior said 'It's two o'clock'
The Roman soldier got a big shock
The Roman soldier said 'Oh my God it's dinner time'
That's the end of a silly rhyme.

Rob Turley (8)
Kader Primary School, Middlesbrough

The Minotaur Haiku

A minotaur waits,
In a dark damp labyrinth
Silent for dinner.

Jack Price (9)
Kader Primary School, Middlesbrough

Water

Water flows in and out,
Water flows round and about.
It makes waves in the river,
It swirls in the lake,
It moves so much it isn't fake
Water helps us all grow,
Is water a friend or is it a foe?
If we didn't have water what would we do?
Water goes in our loo
Water goes in our Coke,
With water you even choke.

Vidya Gosain (7)
Kader Primary School, Middlesbrough

Star A Light

Star a light you shine so bright not even the sun is brighter
Star a light you make the winter night lighter
Your shape is pointy but could not harm anything
Every time you shine I hear a little ting
You make me feel warm inside my cold body
What makes you shine so bright in the night
I wish I could just fly to you and see what makes you shine
Star a light I wish I could be you.

Rebecca Chalk (8)
Kader Primary School, Middlesbrough

Dogs, Mice And Cats

Dogs and cats are always fighting
And they're all really good at biting.
They're always running around the house
And sometimes the cat chases a poor little mouse.
Once upon a time that's what I say
Because now I'm calling it a day.

Emily Holden (8)
Kader Primary School, Middlesbrough

Wish, Wish, Wish

I wish I had an older sister
I wish I could stay up late
I wish I didn't have so many blisters
I wish I had more mates.

I wish I had a new car
I wish I had a new name
I wish I had a twinkling star
I wish and wish all the same.

I wish my mum wasn't called Gill
I wish my sister's name wasn't Emma
I wish I could watch The Bill
I wish I didn't have a dilemma.

I wish I didn't have to work
I wish my grandpa was alive
I wish people didn't smirk
I wish I had a beehive.

Rebecca Briggs (8)
Lingfield Primary School, Middlesbrough

Wish, Wish, Wish

I wish I didn't have two sisters
I wish I was good at sports
I wish I didn't get big blisters
I wish I was in charge of an airport.

I wish school wasn't made
I wish I could do good things at home
I wish I'd get lots when I get paid
I wish we beat the football team Rome.

I wish I had a lot of money
I wish I had a horse called Peter
I wish I had a big brown bunny
I wish I had better heater.

Sam Bytheway (9)
Lingfield Primary School, Middlesbrough

Wish, Wish, Wish

I wish my brother wasn't so small
I wish my cousin wasn't so nasty
I wish my aunty wasn't so tall
I wish my taste buds would like a pasty.

I wish my hair was ever so straight
I wish I was one foot taller
I wish I could have a best mate
I wish my mates were a little bit smaller.

I wish I could score more goals
I wish I had a big, big pool
I wish I had two pet moles
I wish I was a bit more cool.

I wish my friends could come and sleep
I wish I could be famous and rich
I wish I could do a really high leap
I wish I wouldn't get a stitch.

Robyn Bulpitt (9)
Lingfield Primary School, Middlesbrough

Wish, Wish, Wish

I wish my brother was kind to me
I wish our house was built
I wish I had more PlayStation games
I wish I had a puppy.

I wish my mum wouldn't sing
I wish my brother was small
I wish my name was Liam
I wish I was in the Boro team.

I wish I was bigger than my brother
I wish I was both-footed at football
I wish my dad didn't go out all the time
I wish I was better than my brother at football.

Joshua Fox (9)
Lingfield Primary School, Middlesbrough

Wish, Wish, Wish

I wish I could change my bedroom
I wish my cousin wasn't so far
I wish I had a red room
I wish I didn't have to drive a mile in my car.

I wish I didn't have a sister
I wish I had a brother
I wish I didn't have a blister
I wish I had a better mother.

I wish I could score a lot more goals
I wish I could have a pet
I wish I could be like Paul Scholes
I wish I could win a set.

I wish I could change my name
I wish I didn't have a bad cough
I wish I went on a plane
I wish I didn't get sent off.

Andrew Busby (9)
Lingfield Primary School, Middlesbrough

Wish, Wish, Wish

I wish we could have a flood
I wish I was allowed to throw mud
I wish I could have loads of fun
I wish there was no such thing as a gun.

I wish there was no such thing as sauce
I wish I was part of the Royal Air Force
I wish I really did like plums
I wish we didn't have to write sums.

I wish I had a big pet snail
I wish in tests I could never fail
I wish I slept in a red bed
I wish my granddad wasn't dead.

Max Tweddle ((8)
Lingfield Primary School, Middlesbrough

Wish, Wish, Wish

I wish I didn't have something to help me breathe
I wish I didn't have asthma and hayfever too
I wish my sister had a posher name than Eve
I wish my mum's name wasn't Betty-Lou.

I wish I didn't have two pet mole rats
I wish my parents were back together
I wish I didn't get an F in my SATs
I wish I didn't feel like I brought dull weather.

I wish my dad hadn't gone away
I wish he would come to see me
I wish I wouldn't think about him every day
I wish I had a proper family.

I wish I wasn't so alone
I wish my lips weren't blue
I wish I was allowed on the phone
I wish I was someone new!

Ellena Craggy (9)
Lingfield Primary School, Middlesbrough

Wish, Wish, Wish

I wish I could eat ice cream
I wish I had a great dream
I wish for the war to stop
I wish that bunnies could hop
I wish that piggies could fly
I wish wrestlers could tie
I wish there was pretty flowers in school
I wish there was a pool in school
I wish people wouldn't get laughed at
I wish I could play with a bat.

Callum Woodhouse (10)
Lingfield Primary School, Middlesbrough

Wish, Wish, Wish

I wish my brother didn't beat me up
I wish someone except my family liked me
I wish I had a pup
I wish I was full of glee.

I wish I was better at sport
I wish I was more hyperactive
I wish I was never taught
I wish I was more selective.

I wish I was more clever
I wish I had never killed that fish
I wish my brother was Trevor
I wish I had a safari.

I wish I had good ideas
I wish my art work was good all the time
I wish my bike had more gears
I wish my work was always fine.

Adam Davies (9)
Lingfield Primary School, Middlesbrough

Wish, Wish, Wish

I wish my granddad wasn't poorly
I wish I wasn't tone deaf
I wish I had jewellery
I wish my mum was called Steph.

I wish I had a box full of black jacks
I wish I had a red Ferrari
I wish I had ten Big Macs
I wish I was top at karate.

I wish I was a little bit taller
I wish I had more friends
I wish I was a better bowler
I wish I had gel pens.

Mathew Pearson (9)
Lingfield Primary School, Middlesbrough

Wish, Wish, Wish

I wish I was rich and lived in a mansion
But I like being normal better
I wish I wouldn't feel so bad
It makes me feel like an unopened letter.

I wish no one would ever die
Because I want my family to be with me
I wish I could last a hundred years
And have a son at twenty.

I wish I was an actor
But probably not I'm too fat
I wish I wasn't so left out
It's like being a doormat.

I wish, I wish, I don't know what to wish
My wish is falling like a feather
But my biggest wish of all is for you to come back
And stay with me forever and ever and ever.

Tabby Hicks (9)
Lingfield Primary School, Middlesbrough

The Moon

The moon is like a luminous light
Sometimes it shines very bright
It could even light up the streets
But it won't have any control over who he meets.

The moon helps us sleep
He makes it dark all over the town
But sometimes he has a little frown
He sees crimes and can't calm down.

The moon can be happy, the moon can be sad
It depends what he feels like
But most of all he likes watching us asleep.

Lucy Taylor (9)
Lingfield Primary School, Middlesbrough

Wish, Wish, Wish

I wish my brother wouldn't hit me
I wish my baby sister wouldn't scratch
I wish I didn't have a bumpy knee
I wish people wouldn't snatch.

I wish I would never be late
I wish my hair never got in knots
I wish I would smash a plate
I wish I will never get spots.

I wish my dogs wouldn't scratch me
I wish my mum wouldn't cut my hair so short
I wish I liked coffee and tea
I wish I never got caught.

I wish I could do a back flip
I wish my mum wouldn't shout
I wish I could go on a big dip
I wish I always hung about.

Isabel Humphreys (9)
Lingfield Primary School, Middlesbrough

The Moon

The moon is looking down on Earth,
With a great big smile,
It's waiting to be landed on,
As it sits and stares for a while.
The moon is shining brightly,
Still looking down on Earth,
Its attention then turns to the stars,
All squashed together tightly.
The moon stands out in the dark night sky
Shining merrily
Till morning is nigh.

Jessica Edwards (10)
Lingfield Primary School, Middlesbrough

Wish, Wish, Wish

I wish I never had a sister
I wish I had a parrot
I wish I never had a bad knee
I wish I was better at drawing.

I wish I was better at motor cross
I wish I could go to the moon
I wish I was good at archery
I wish I went to university.

I wish I was better at holding my hamster
I wish I had a brother
I wish I could go on holiday
I wish I could live in a mansion.

I wish I had a dog
I wish I was famous
I wish I was an actor
I wish I had a limousine.

I wish I could hit my target with my bow and arrows
I wish I could live forever
I wish I was twenty years old
I wish I could stay up late.

Jack Hunter (9)
Lingfield Primary School, Middlesbrough

The Moon

The moon is as silver as the Carling Cup,
It is surrounded by total darkness,
So its twinkle stands out better.
The moon is a giant football
When the moon is crescent it looks like a banana,
The moon must be happy in the sky
When there is a total eclipse
I see the shadow of the moon.

Robert Kerr (9)
Lingfield Primary School, Middlesbrough

Wish, Wish, Wish

I wish I had dark brown hair
I wish I could play my violin well
I wish my sister would care
I wish I could wash my hair with gel.

I wish I had another pet
I wish I liked macaroni
I wish I wouldn't fret
I wish I had a pony.

I wish I had a computer
I wish my friend came round
I wish I could see to the future
I wish I didn't feel like a hunted hound.

I wish I could swim
I wish I could get a cat
I wish I could win
I wish I could act.

Sally Ivison (9)
Lingfield Primary School, Middlesbrough

The Moon

The moon is a bright bulb
Gazing over the world saying
'Welcome' to all that hear,
Smiling all night long, with
His big silver eyes looking
Around.

The moon is like a crystal,
Hanging over the sky to give
Light, it is like a face that
Smiles all the time, so
Whenever you look out at
Night you will see the moon
Up in the sky.

Alice Blott (10)
Lingfield Primary School, Middlesbrough

Wish, Wish, Wish

I wish I could go for a run with my dad
I wish my skin wasn't so sensitive
I wish I could be good at science so I could be glad
I wish Jess my dog would win fly ball.

I wish I wouldn't always trip and fall
I wish my mum and dad didn't argue
I wish my grandad would come back to this world
I wish Beth could come for a long stay.

I wish my bedroom was blue
I wish I had another snail
I wish there was no such thing as flu
I wish my cat was not a male.

I wish my dog wouldn't cower at every loud noise
I wish my grandma's weren't so dopey
I wish I could see the horse Boize
I wish, wish, wish my life wasn't full of mistakes.

Mina Jackson (9)
Lingfield Primary School, Middlesbrough

The Moon

When I was small I used to say,
'I want to go to the moon.'
My mother replied in a reassuring voice,
'You may go one day, but not soon.'
I am ten years old now and I still have that dream
That one day, just maybe, I may be seen on the moon
Up in the stars amongst the planets Pluto and Mars
That fantasy will stay with me forever that old lifelong dream
That one day I may visit my good friend, the moon!

Alex Dampier (10)
Lingfield Primary School, Middlesbrough

Wish, Wish, Wish

I wish my hair was blonde and black
I wish I was twenty-one
I wish I would never pack
I wish my homework was done.

I wish I could stay up late
I wish I was good at football
I wish I could play with my mate
I wish I could play in a big hall.

I wish I didn't go to school
I wish I could go to the shops
I wish Middlesbrough beat Liverpool
I wish I had cricket tops.

I wish I had a PS2
I wish I could go to the cinema
I wish I had a proper snooker cue
I wish, I wish, I wish!

Andrew Harland (9)
Lingfield Primary School, Middlesbrough

The Moon

When I look at the moon
It reminds me of a little ball of butter
The moon comes out at night to play
But hides at day
It rolls across the sky
For no reason, why?
When I look up at the man in the moon
I wonder, why does he run from the big warm sun?

Matthew Clarke (10)
Lingfield Primary School, Middlesbrough

Wish, Wish, Wish

I wish my hair went right down my back
I wish my bedroom was so much bigger
I wish my sister didn't always wear black
I wish I could jump as high as Tigger.

I wish my friends could come and sleep
I wish for school I wasn't often late
I wish my dad wasn't always sleeping so deep
I wish my two front teeth were straight.

I wish my socks weren't full of holes
I wish my dog didn't scratch
I wish my shoes had comfy soles
I wish I could find socks to match.

I wish I was better at sports like footie
I wish I didn't have to flush my fish
I wish my sister wasn't nutty
I wish a wish would help me wish.

Abbie McDonald (9)
Lingfield Primary School, Middlesbrough

The Moon

The moon is as round as a ball of snow, hanging from the
                                        inky-black sky
The moon calls out 'Welcome' and gives a dreamy sigh,
The moon glows like a shimmering, shining star
He whispers to all 'Don't worry, I'm not very far'
The moon looks down upon the Earth, with gleaming silver eyes
I will always, always say to people the moonlight never dies
The moon represents the world
I dream about it as I'm lying in my bed all tightly curled
So, always remember the moon will forever be with us
Bear that in mind . . . my mam does.

Jessica Watts (10)
Lingfield Primary School, Middlesbrough

Wish, Wish, Wish

I wish I was called Thiery Henry
I wish I had an older sister
I wish I had my own tree
I wish I didn't have a blister.

I wish I had my own car
I wish my sister was nice
I wish I could drive to the Spar
I wish I could roll a dice.

I wish I had lots of money
I wish I had another horse
I wish I had a lot of honey
I wish I could run on a racecourse.

I wish I went on holiday
I wish I had another dog
I wish I could have a sunny day
I wish I had a sitting log.

Alan Milburn (9)
Lingfield Primary School, Middlesbrough

The Moon

The moon has a shape like Big Ben's face.
The moon is a bauble jingling on a sleigh.
The moon is as big as a fluffy white cloud.
The moon is very quiet, not very loud.
The moon is as shiny as a new dance floor.
The moon is bigger than a door.
The moon shines brightly down all night.
The moon is like a star falling.
The moon is whiter than a set of false teeth.

The shining light is shining, lit like a candle.
Frosty skylight covers the sky.
Clouds moving across it.
The moon is sailing through the night.
The moon is important.

Jade Burton (10)
Lingfield Primary School, Middlesbrough

The Sea

A swirling whirling monster
Crashing waves
Rocks being hurled upon the sand
Ship-drowning beast
Calm ocean waves
Gentle splashes
Laughing children
Relaxed like a well trained pet
Home to sharks
Jellyfish and squid
Lair of a powerful force
Life-claiming and ruthless
Changing like a person's mood
Gentle and fierce
Still and calm
Angry and thrashing
Treasure holder
Keeper of many secrets
A sunken world of mysteries
Holder of many dangers
A worldwide wonder
Destroyer of calmness
Soother of anger
This is the sea.

Megan Iley (10)
Lingfield Primary School, Middlesbrough

The Moon

One night in June I saw the moon
The moon was as big as a giant prune.
It was shaped like an orange, it was as bright as a light,
But when I went out there was no moon in sight.
The moon is like a cat's eye
We all say the moon will never die.

Alice Smith (10)
Lingfield Primary School, Middlesbrough

Wish, Wish, Wish

I wish I didn't look like my sisters
I wish my brother was nice
I wish I didn't get blisters
I wish my granddad played with a dice.

I wish my grandma was alive
I wish I had a gran
I wish my granddad could jive
I wish my granddad ran.

I wish I didn't have cold sores
I wish I had blonde hair
I wish I ate two apple cores
I wish I could go to a funfair.

I wish my mum wouldn't embarrass people
I wish my uncle would not crush me on to the settee
I wish I saw a steeple
I wish I could watch stupid people on TV.

Georgina Nicholls (8)
Lingfield Primary School, Middlesbrough

The Moon

One night in May,
My mother used to say
'Look at the moon
Shining like a silver spoon.'

The moon was as round as a football,
The clouds were like walls
The moon was shining yellow
It looked down on us all.

Conor Spencer (9)
Lingfield Primary School, Middlesbrough

Wish, Wish, Wish

I wish I had a brother
I wish I was Thiery Henry
I wish I was another person
I wish I wasn't me.

I wish I could write in pen
I wish I was the best
I wish I could have a hen
I wish I had lots of friends as a guest.

I wish I was the strongest man in the world
I wish I could fly
I wish I could curl up like a cat
I wish I never cried.

I wish I had a dog
I wish I had Rothchild's money
I wish I had a gold log
I wish the bees would bring me honey.

Sam Pearson (9)
Lingfield Primary School, Middlesbrough

The Moon

One day in May,
I went out to play and I thought . . .
The moon is like the face of a giant clown.
The moon is looking down on us all night long.
The moon lives in a white fluffy place in the sky.
The moon is a great luminous glow stick floating in the sky.
The moon is looking down on us with his great marble eyes.
The moon is smiling at us with a great big grin.
The moon is a great big orange.

Stephanie Barker (10)
Lingfield Primary School, Middlesbrough

The Moon

The moon shines high in the sky
Like a big glowing pie
The moon in the sky.

Hello moon glaring down
With that face like a clown,
The moon in the sky.

As it eats passing stars
It also sits and stares at Mars,
The moon in the sky.

As round as a ping pong ball
On it not a tree or wall,
The moon in the sky.

The moon is like a giant light
Shining on the earth so bright,
The moon in the sky.

Matthew Emery (10)
Lingfield Primary School, Middlesbrough

Wish, Wish, Wish

I wish I had more friends
I wish I didn't have any brothers
I wish my name was Lucy
I wish I didn't go to school.

I wish I had four sisters that were nice to me
I wish people were nice to me
I wish I didn't get shouted at by my mother and father.

I wish I went on holiday from home
I wish I had lots of money to buy stuff.

Laura Readman (8)
Lingfield Primary School, Middlesbrough

Wish, Wish, Wish

I wish I didn't get bullied
I wish I wasn't afraid or sick
I wish I wasn't always buried
I wish everyone stopped punching and kicking.

I wish I had a few more friends
I wish I could go to the zoo
I wish I could see some red hens
I wish I could see some blue bottomed monkeys too.

I wish I could be famous
I wish I was more clever
I wish my name was Seamus
I wish I was popular forever.

I wish I was rich
I wish I had a limousine
I wish I can stop falling in a ditch
I wish my face was pale not green.

Alex Hatfield (9)
Lingfield Primary School, Middlesbrough

No Word Of A Lie

I'm the best at dance and that's
No word of a lie
We always ski in France and that's
No word of a lie
I can always tell when people are going to cry and that's
No word of a lie
My mum is the world's best and most famous spy and that's
No word of a lie!

Chloe Whitby (8)
Lingfield Primary School, Middlesbrough

Wish, Wish, Wish

I wish I had blonde long hair
I wish it would swing in the air
I wish my sister was fair
I wish I could not care.

I wish I had no freckles
They are brown and black and grey
I wish I did not fall on nettles
I wish to have a baby in May.

I wish I was part of a crew
I wish I could sail on a ship
I wish my name was Pru
I wish cars did not go pip.

I wish cows did not go moo
I wish they did not go chew, chew, chew
I wish I saw a cow that was blue
I wish cows would wear shoes.

Claire Everitt (9)
Lingfield Primary School, Middlesbrough

No Word Of A Lie

I have a pet fox and that's
No word of a lie
I have a collection of the world's largest rocks and that's
No word of a lie
Whenever I want, I can make it snow and that's
No word of a lie
I am always happy and never low and that's
No word of a lie.

Isabel Carruthers (8)
Lingfield Primary School, Middlesbrough

No Word Of A Lie

I am the best person to fly in the sky and that's
No word of a lie
My mum makes the best apple pie and that's
No word of a lie
I am the best in school at running and that's
No word of a lie
I have a golden fox who is very cunning and that's
No word of a lie.

Alexandra Walker (8)
Lingfield Primary School, Middlesbrough

Rockabaloosa

A man and a woman met at the park.
Under the moonlight listening to a lark.
They sat on a bench and looked at the moon
And then they kissed, all too soon
Rockabaloosa!
The moon shines bright
Like a glistening diamond in the night.

Kieran Woodhouse (10)
Lingfield Primary School, Middlesbrough

The Moon

The moon is like a parent looking down on the child.
The child is the Earth and the parent is the moon.
He looks on him at night but in day he says
'I'll see you soon'
Now that's our bright shining moon.

Dale Scurr (10)
Lingfield Primary School, Middlesbrough

No Word Of A Lie

I have the world's biggest diamond ring and that's
No word of a lie
I have a magical harp and it goes ping and that's
No word of a lie
I have a limousine that's all my own and that's
No word of a lie
My dog has its own dinosaur bone and that's
No word of a lie.

Olivia Thompson (8)
Lingfield Primary School, Middlesbrough

The Moon

The moon is a big white ball.
The moon is a big white egg.
The moon is a flying spaceship.
The moon is a glowing light.
The moon is as round as an apple.
The moon is as fat as a snowball.
The moon smiles down on us all.

Dale Readman (10)
Lingfield Primary School, Middlesbrough

The Moon

The moon is a big ball of butter
The moon is looking down on Earth
The moon is the shape of a fingernail
The moon is the colour of a banana
The moon shines like a piece of gold.

Jordan Spencer (9)
Lingfield Primary School, Middlesbrough

No Word Of A Lie

I am best friends with Ganesh and that's
No word of a lie
I have a town house in Bangladesh and that's
No word of a lie
I heard a pencil talk and that's
No word of a lie
And on water I can walk and that's
No word of a lie.

Benjamin Learwood (8)
Lingfield Primary School, Middlesbrough

No Word Of A Lie

My mum's landed on Pluto twice and that's
No word of a lie
I eat sandwiches made of mice and that's
No word of a lie
I've read a Harry Potter book which isn't out and that's
No word of a lie
I have a warthog with the world's longest snout and that's
No word of a lie.

Sam Peirson (8)
Lingfield Primary School, Middlesbrough

No Word Of A Lie

I can't tell when I'm going to burst and that's
No word of a lie
I know when somebody is cursed and that's
No word of a lie
I have a villa in sunny Spain and that's
No word of a lie
I always travel on a private jet plane and that's
No word of a lie.

Elliot Duffy (8)
Lingfield Primary School, Middlesbrough

No Word Of A Lie

I have got the world's biggest ted and that's
No word of a lie
I have the world's brainiest head and that's
No word of a lie
I can make loads of money and that's
No word of a lie
My bees make the best honey and that's
No word of a lie.

Thomas Matthews (8)
Lingfield Primary School, Middlesbrough

No Word Of A Lie

I live in a palace and that's
No word of a lie
I went to Wonderland and met Alice and that's
No word of a lie
I have a pet polar bear and that's
No word of a lie
I have the best coloured hair and that's
No word of a lie.

Katie Parkes (8)
Lingfield Primary School, Middlesbrough

No Word Of A Lie

I know that I am so skilful and that's
No word of a lie
My dad thinks it's good to be wilful and that's
No word of a lie
I always roll a six on the dice and that's
No word of a lie
We are millionaires and we buy lots of rice and that's
No word of a lie.

John Phellas (8)
Lingfield Primary School, Middlesbrough

No Word Of A Lie

I have the world's oldest books and that's
No word of a lie
I am allergic to ducks and that's
No word of a lie
My hair is really, really curled and that's
No word of a lie
Six times I've been around the world and that's
No word of a lie.

Eve Craggy (8)
Lingfield Primary School, Middlesbrough

No Word Of A Lie

I have a dog with two heads and that's
No word of a lie
I got five bunk beds and that's
No word of a lie
I have ten flying pigs and that's
No word of a lie
I never lose when I play tigs and that's
No word of a lie.

Jade Taylor (8)
Lingfield Primary School, Middlesbrough

The Moon

The moon is a huge hole, burning its way through the sky.
The moon is a clock face, ticking its way through time.
The moon is a fingernail, scratching the stars and sky.
The moon is a dinner plate, hanging on a black draining board.
The moon is a volleyball, waiting to be hit.

Jenny Craggy (10)
Lingfield Primary School, Middlesbrough

Spring, Summer, Autumn, Winter

Spring, summer, autumn, winter,
Touched wood and got a splinter.
Now the splinter has all gone,
I can't get rid of this awful pong!

Spring, summer, autumn, winter,
I saw a burglar going inter
A house full of goods,
He then came out with two flower buds!

Spring, summer, autumn, winter,
I met a man, he was a hinter.
He dropped a hint,
And lost his flint!

Rachel Sykes (11)
Northgate Junior School, Guisborough

I Wish

I wish I was a cowboy
So I could round up all the cattle
I'd ride on horses all the time
Even have a battle.

I wish I was a spaceman
So I could float around the universe
I'd fly to different planets
Hey, what could be worse?

But I think I'll stay myself today
Perhaps another day
I'll find a way.

James Bowes (11)
Northgate Junior School, Guisborough

I Wish I Had A Dog

All my friends, they have a dog and always play with them,
They never play out with me,
Their dog comes first,
Why can't my parents see?
I wish I had a dog.

We were asked to draw our pet at school
All I drew was a single fish.
Having a dog would be so cool,
If only my parents knew what I wish.
Because I wish I had a dog.

My birthday is coming up soon,
And I thought I would get a dog.
I got a packet of bobbles, water bombs and a balloon,
I moaned and I moaned and I moaned and I moaned,
But I still never got a dog.

Natasha Dickinson (10)
Northgate Junior School, Guisborough

My Friend

My friend is always there for me
Wherever I may be
Through thick and thin
She will bring,
Just a treat for me.
The sun shining
I am whining
And she will make a joke
Just like her folks
Her name is Rachel
And she's a little angel.

Sophie Crawford (10)
Northgate Junior School, Guisborough

My Mum

My mum works at my school
She is rather cool.
She's a dinner lady,
So she goes outside.
She loves to be in places,
Where it's shady.
My mam helps little kids
When they cry.
She sits them down on a bench
And asks them 'Why?'
She shouts at naughty kids,
They begin to cry.
She says, 'That won't wash with me
So there's no need to try!'

Eleanor Matthews (9)
Northgate Junior School, Guisborough

Boro

M ighty and strong in every game
 I dol to me and many others
D ecisive goals nearly every game
D esperate points needed
L eaving teams victorious
E urope here we come
S lashing Bolton, Man U, Arsenal, Leeds
B etter players every season
R iverside roaring
O n loan players
U nited we stay
G oals pouring
H ero he stays, Steve Gibson.

James Mayhew (11)
Northgate Junior School, Guisborough

My Dad

My dad is *great!*
He is always there for me,
When you want to find him you will always know where to go.
Off we go to the bookies!
He also likes a good old pint.
He is getting a few grey hairs
But sill who cares?
He is still my *dad!*

Jade Clements (11)
Northgate Junior School, Guisborough

Family

Fun-loving sisters like Jessica,
Amazing mums like Mandy,
Messy bedrooms tidied by Mum
Inspiring dogs like Cindy,
Loving dads like Eddie,
Years of fun have just begun!

Aimee Bruerton (11)
Northgate Junior School, Guisborough

My Sister

My sister is funny and is always smiling,
You can always trust her even when she is dying!
When you are in trouble she will be there to help,
Even when her child is teething and she yelps!
But sometimes she picks on me so you'll sometimes find me crying!

Lauren Smith (10)
Northgate Junior School, Guisborough

Ghosts

G hostly ghouls
H orrifying,
O ver there in the graveyard,
S ouls from the dead,
T errifying,
S uffering spirits.

Carl Reid (11)
Northgate Junior School, Guisborough

My Nanna

Kind lover
House cleaner
Forgiver
Caring Nanna
Friendly person
Slow mover.

Dane Matthewman (11)
Northgate Junior School, Guisborough

My Friend Jade

My friend Jade
Went on holiday with a bucket and spade.
When she got back,
She had to unpack,
That's my friend Jade.

Stacy Williams (11)
Northgate Junior School, Guisborough

Animals

A nimals, loving and caring
N ature is wonderful, special and sharing,
I n our world the animal grows
M aking daffodil chains it seems like we sew,
A nimals, beautiful petals so thin,
L ingering right down, their stems like a pin
S leeping softly, the night begins.

Simone Wye (10)
Northgate Junior School, Guisborough

Ghosts

G hosts are freaky
H aunting houses is their job
O nce it's night-time they appear
S wift and invisible they are
T hey sleep in the day and come out at night
S hould we run or should we hide?

Lewis Johnson (11)
Northgate Junior School, Guisborough

Sports

S ports are great to me
P eople can play for free
O n a Tuesday night
R eal fun but sometimes we fight
T op team I guarantee
S cored more goals than twenty-three.

Eleanor Hewson (11)
Northgate Junior School, Guisborough

My Dog

My dog is strong and big
His name is Joe and he likes to dig
He's a bulldog and he licks his nose
We also clean him with a great big hose
We play all day and we never have a break
Although we have to stop for some tasty steak
We love our dog Joe
But we have to let him go
And see him tomorrow.

Rachel Wallace (11)
Northgate Junior School, Guisborough

Oceans

Curves and waves the ocean's glaze
On the summer daze.

But then we heard a crash and blaze
Here was the end of the summer daze.

And now comes snow that sparkles low
On the sand where children go.

Chelsee Breeze (11)
Northgate Junior School, Guisborough

Autumn

A ll the leaves start to fall,
U nder the coldness of the sky the trees grow tall.
T ime goes by and leaves come back,
U p like a sprout the leaves come back
M ists fill the sky,
N ow autumn comes and the leaves start to die.

Chelsea Skidmore (11)
Northgate Junior School, Guisborough

Stormy Seas

Like a wolf howling in the night.
Fierce and cunning
Like a mighty beast
Which roars on the rocks
It makes a black sky
The vicious clouds
Start to blow in with the dreadful wind.
It rips the sails and the boat starts to fall apart.

Jordan Corner (9)
Northgate Junior School, Guisborough

Fathers

F athers are caring
A re always around
T here for you when you are feeling sick or down
H appy and always smiling
E verything imagined, imagine him not being there
R espectful and understanding
S o love your dad and care for him while he is around.

Tyler Wedgwood (11)
Northgate Junior School, Guisborough

Summer

S ummer sun lights up the sky,
U sually when people are walking by.
M any people get a tan in summer,
M en and women get really hot and get a bit glummer.
E veryone lies on the grass,
R ising sun is a big ball of gas.

Lucy Storey (11)
Northgate Junior School, Guisborough

Sweets

I don't like different types of meats
The only thing I like is sweets.
I eat them sour when I'm in the shower,
I eat them sweet when I'm walking down the street.
Sweets can be red, sweets can be blue
I also like the green ones too.
Whether they're round, whether they're square
Thin or fat, I just don't care.
After my tea, after my lunch,
I have sweets for a little munch,
Ones in wrappers, sticks of rock,
Sometimes I hide them in my sock.

Jessica Williams (10)
Northgate Junior School, Guisborough

Yum, Yuck!

I like bangers and mash,
I don't like corned beef and tattie hash.
I love cheese,
But not green peas.

I like kebab,
I don't like crab.
I love toffee,
But not coffee!

Clare Peacock (9)
Northgate Junior School, Guisborough

Matty

There was a boy called Matty
Who really was batty
He climbed a tree
And fell on his knee
And now he is unhappy.

Sam Thompson (11)
Northgate Junior School, Guisborough

Grey Mouse

In a field so far away,
There lived a mouse, so small and grey.
He had a nose so cute and sweet,
And fast flat toes upon his feet.

All day long he would look for food,
Red berries and leaves depending on his mood.
He would sit and eat alone,
And not once would grey mouse moan.

Then one day he saw in a dream,
A beauty, a wonder, a love supreme.
He opened his eyes and scratched his head,
A little brown mouse was sat on his bed.

It wasn't a dream, but a beautiful vision,
This mouse was alive wanting provisions.
She was lonely and hungry and had no clothes,
So grey mouse hugged her and rubbed her nose.

They live happily now, together as one,
Sharing tea and biscuits, berries and scones.
They are warm and cosy in their big brown house,
With room enough for a little brown mouse.

Ashley Fairburn (10)
Pallister Park Primary School, Middlesbrough

The Toy Train

This is the toy train under the bed,
Dodge the wardrobe and through the fake shed.
Faster and faster, here it comes,
Mind out for your fingers and thumbs.
Past the lamp,
Up the ramp
And . . .
Crashhhh!

Gabrielle Sadler-Hunt (9)
Pallister Park Primary School, Middlesbrough

My Gran

She sleeps like a baby,
Her hair is like cotton wool,
She sits all hunched and baggy,
She looks like a queen.

She works like an engine,
Her eyes are like sapphires,
She cackles when she laughs,
She is as funny as a clown.

She talks non stop,
She smokes like a train,
She is the best,
I love her.

Bethany Williamson (10)
Pallister Park Primary School, Middlesbrough

The Train

I am a train
I go fast and slow
Over hills high
And through valleys low
Rushing past houses
Here I go
With a clickety clack
And a whistle I go.

Jack Banks (10)
Pallister Park Primary School, Middlesbrough

Accident

She ate a fish,
She ate a sweet,
She ate a sandwich,
Then slipped on some meat!

Ryan Jones (7)
Pallister Park Primary School, Middlesbrough

Things About Friends

Friends are helpful,
Friends are kind,
They clear bad things off your mind.
They're always there when you're unwell,
Oh what friends they are!

Friends are loving,
Friends are caring,
They never mind what you're wearing,
They take you everywhere they go,
Their answer is always yes! Not no! No! No!

Chloe McElwee (10)
Pallister Park Primary School, Middlesbrough

The Toy Box Train

Into the toy box which belongs to Jack,
And all along the big toy track.
Along and along to pick up Mr Pup
Past the big, blue, dusty cup.
Getting slower up the ramp,
Bridges over and past the lamp.
Over the big, black chalkboard
Under the deep blue and gold toy sword.
The . . . end . . . of . . . the . . . bed,
We all arrive home with a sleepy head.

Tasmin Bowes-Chester (10)
Pallister Park Primary School, Middlesbrough

She Fell In The Pie

She jumped over a house,
She jumped over a slide,
She jumped over a swing,
Then fell in a pie!

Cameron Corner (7)
Pallister Park Primary School, Middlesbrough

The Express Train

Here we are waiting at the station
People wait for their destination
Here is the train coming this way
To make it an excellent day

Suddenly it comes to a halt
Everyone scrambles through the door
People walking up and down
Trying to find seats.

The whistle blows, off the train sets
People chatting, eating and drinking
Sleeping as the train sets off for beautiful Spain.

Adam Pirie (9)
Pallister Park Primary School, Middlesbrough

Railway

R eady and roaring to get on the train
A nyone and everyone is excited.
I n the tunnel it was inky-black.
L augher is in the air.
W hen we got off the train I was excited.
A ll of the people I could see were ready for their holiday.
Y ou and me are ready to see our destination.

Leah McClelland (9)
Pallister Park Primary School, Middlesbrough

Summer Comes

Summer comes
With flowers growing
Summer comes
With the sunshine shining
Summer comes
With children playing.

Gemma Parkin (8)
Pallister Park Primary School, Middlesbrough

Steam Train

Steam trains pass by
They're going so fast I think they will fly
Everyone coughs from the steam
I think trains are really mean
More trains come into the station
Thousands more people get to their destination
Round the bend comes the train
And now no one can complain
In a flash I'm in my seat
Now I can relax and put up my feet.

Lloyd Evans (9)
Pallister Park Primary School, Middlesbrough

The Train

The train is inky-black.
Hear the coal being shovelled into the tube train.
Everything is dark.

The train is beginning to stop.
Usually the train stops very slowly.
But everyone was amazed . . .
This one stopped incredibly fast.

Corrinna Richards (10)
Pallister Park Primary School, Middlesbrough

Jumping Girl

She jumped over a house,
She jumped over a fish,
She jumped over a door,
She fell in a dish!

Chelsea Smyth (7)
Pallister Park Primary School, Middlesbrough

The Girl Who Ate

She ate a sweet,
She ate a fish,
She ate a pie,
Then she got a dish.

She ate a pancake,
She ate a plum
She ate an apple,
And then she did her sums.

Abigail Davies (7)
Pallister Park Primary School, Middlesbrough

Clumsy Girl

She ate a pear,
She ate a plum
She ate a banana,
And she hurt her bum.

She ate some crisps,
She ate a fish,
She ate a fish finger,
And broke a dish!

Curtis Robinson (7)
Pallister Park Primary School, Middlesbrough

Ding-Ping!

She ate a chip,
She ate a string,
She ate some peas,
Then said, 'Ding-ping!'

She ate a hair,
She ate some custard,
She ate a lolly,
And said 'Mustard!'

Abbie Morris (7)
Pallister Park Primary School, Middlesbrough

Friends

Look around,
What can be found,
With a friend in your imagination.
Always there to show they care.
Never letting you down,
Those are the best friends that can be found.

They're always around but don't make a sound
Because . . .
They are only in your imagination.
If you could only find a true friend
You wouldn't need to
Imagine.

Ashleigh Ingledew (10)
Pallister Park Primary School, Middlesbrough

Steam Train

S tanding at the station waiting
T rain arriving, going to our destination
E xcited and nervous
A rriving at the place,
M eeting new people, learning their name

T ravelling to Cardiff on the steam train
R ushing to the football match
A ngry England fans waiting for the train
I nky-black in the tunnel
N obody can see anything when they look out of the window.

Lindsey McClelland (9)
Pallister Park Primary School, Middlesbrough

The Great Train Of Light

We're all going on a train
So we don't get caught in the rain
All is well and clear
My dad's got a can of beer
We're not at the station
We are waiting for our destination
My feet are going to follow the beat
Of the train and the rain.

Our journey has almost come to an end
As we sway round the bend
We get off the train
And end up as wet as a drain.

Amy Matthews (10)
Pallister Park Primary School, Middlesbrough

Winter Comes

Winter comes
With snow drifting
Winter comes
With the wind blowing
Winter comes
With frost
Winter comes
With children playing
Winter comes
With children shouting.

Chantelle Smyth (9)
Pallister Park Primary School, Middlesbrough

Winter Comes

Winter comes
With the snow falling
Winter comes
With the children playing snowballing
Winter comes
With the wind blowing
Winter comes
With the snowflakes falling
Winter comes
With people sliding
Winter comes
With the fire burning.

Bethany Cronin (9)
Pallister Park Primary School, Middlesbrough

Summer Comes

Summer comes
With flowers growing
Summer comes
With sun shining
Summer comes
With people tanning
Summer comes
With bees buzzing
Summer comes
With children playing.

Nicole Llewellyn (8)
Pallister Park Primary School, Middlesbrough

Dawn

Dawn comes
With birds twittering.
Dawn comes
With mail man whistling.
Dawn comes
With people waking.
Dawn comes
With the kettle shaking.
Dawn comes
With dogs barking.
Dawn comes
With people talking.

Jennifer Thomas (9)
Pallister Park Primary School, Middlesbrough

Summer

Summer comes
With flowers growing
Summer comes
With a little breeze flowing
Summer comes
With people tanning
Summer comes
With sandcastles growing
Summer comes
With the sun shining!

Georgia Smith (8)
Pallister Park Primary School, Middlesbrough

Evening Comes

Evening comes
With the sky darkening
Evening comes
With the sun setting
Dawn comes
With the sun rising
Dawn comes
With the sky lightening.

Beth Byrne (9)
Pallister Park Primary School, Middlesbrough

Autumn

Autumn comes
With tree leaves falling
Autumn comes
With a breeze that is freezing
Autumn comes
With people shivering
Autumn comes
With early nights.

Lyndsey Coleman (9)
Pallister Park Primary School, Middlesbrough

Tigers

T igers are stripy
I guanas have long noses
G orillas are black and they pat their chests
E lephants have long trunks
R ainforests, animals living everywhere
S nakes are long and they slither.

Rachael Turnbull (9)
Red Rose Primary School, Chester-Le-Street

A Great Holiday

Lanzaroté was great!
Relaxing in the pool,
Going for long walks down the beach,
The sparkling sea,
And the golden sand,
Views from windows and cliff tops
The colourful new land,
Lanzaroté was great!
The hot sun pouring over
The bright green gardens,
Crystal waterfalls,
Tumbling down over the vast rock wall,
Lanzaroté was great!
But one thing that everyone hated,
Was the bugs!
They'd crawl everywhere,
Even in our mugs!
They had to go.
They got caught in the swimming towels,
All over the balcony,
But apart from that . . .
Lanzaroté was great!
There was a family of cats,
That would walk around the café,
We would feed them when they got near,
I'm glad I'm here,
We'd thought quite sad when we packed our cases,
To get on the plane back home again,
But I knew, that in my memory,
A constant reminder, that . . .
Lanzaroté was great!

Holly Gardner (10)
Red Rose Primary School, Chester-Le-Street

Sledging

At Christmas time if I am lucky it will snow.
If it does snow then I'll shout,
'Yeah Mam, Dad, it's snowing!'
I would rush upstairs, clean my teeth
And put on some lovely warm clothes.
Ask my dad if he could take me out to the field
Because we have a massive field down my street.
Then I would run out, open my garage and get out my sledge
And me and my dad would walk down to the field.
Well, I won't be walking!
My dad will be pulling me along in my sledge.
On the field I would go to the top where there is a massive hill
And that's where I'll slide down on my sledge.
'Whoopppeee!'
I would shout.
At the end of the day I would go back home,
If the snow's still there tomorrow I would go back.

Sarah Whitehouse (10)
Red Rose Primary School, Chester-Le-Street

Alice

I was counting the days till September
When my little friend Alice would come.
On the 27th she came
And was here to stay
Her little blue eyes, her soft silky skin made me
Feel like the luckiest girl in the world.
I counted the days till September
That wonderful day I remember,
That wonderful day in September.

Sarah Jones (10)
Red Rose Primary School, Chester-Le-Street

Fighting The Future

On Saturday morning my mum told me
I was going to live in Newcastle.
I was shocked
'Will we see our family again?'
'Yes of course, in the holidays.'
I didn't want to go but it was the best thing that happened in my life.
Six hours it took
As we got to our new house
There I stood,
Still frightened.
The next day was my first day of school
I cried for my mum for a few weeks.
Sometimes my mum had to pick me up from school.
But four years later,
Right now,
I'm happy.
Really, really
Happy.

Abbie Davis (9)
Red Rose Primary School, Chester-Le-Street

My First Time On A Horse

My first time on a horse, was in Scotland,
His name was Max.
I was very scared and tried to relax.
I started to cry
And thought, why oh why am I crying?
Hey! This is not so bad,
I can get used to this
And now I'm not so nervous to get on a horse,
'Cause now that special memory will stay in my head forever,
Of course!

Philippa Attle (10)
Red Rose Primary School, Chester-Le-Street

Lanzaroté

I often go on holidays,
Last time I went to Lanzaroté,
For two whole weeks in the sun.
I had a great time
And lots of fun.
The first day we went to our hotel,
The next few days we went to the pool, to play.
We played
All day
In the sun.
The shallow end of the pool was cold,
But the deep end was hot.
We liked it there,
So we went there a lot.
Other days we went to the beach,
All of us liked playing in the sea
And on the rocks,
Especially me.
I had an ice-lolly,
So did my two sisters Lucy,
And Holly.
And that's why I had the best time ever,
And loads of fun,
Playing all day,
In the sun.

Megan Gardner (10)
Red Rose Primary School, Chester-Le-Street

Witches Wood

We didn't see witches
In Witch Wood,
But we saw
Where the witches had been.

We saw footprints in soft mud
That could only have been used
By some kind of witch.

We saw big trees
Which seemed to be
Looking straight at you.

We saw burnt brooms all around
We saw cats dung
Rolled into balls.

And on trees were dead cats,
We saw burnt bones,
Still very warm.

We didn't see witches
In Witch Wood
But this was the closest
We'd ever been
To believing.

Paul Roll (10)
Red Rose Primary School, Chester-Le-Street

The Ghost Hut

In the Ghost Hut
But we saw
Where the ghosts had been.

We saw scuff marks along the walls
That could only have been scratched
By the great ghosts that haunt the walls
Of the Ghost Hut.

We saw blood-red knives
Which those invisible creatures
Had used whilst stalking throughout
The night.

We saw a skull lying on a red cushion
Watching every step you take
We saw a tomb surrounded by
Delicate, glistening cobwebs.

And hanging from the ceiling was a
Giant, yet pale breath-taking
Human head.

We didn't see ghosts
In the Ghost Hut
But this was the closest
We'd ever been
To seeing.

Katie Miller (10)
Red Rose Primary School, Chester-Le-Street

Goblin Mountain

We didn't see goblins
On Goblin Mountain
But we saw
Where the goblins had been.

We saw three-toed goblin feet
In the yellow sand
That could have only been made
By the goblins.

We saw green shredded skin
That had fallen from the goblin's back
And some hung from the rocks.

We saw a beast's bone
Lying by a red-hot fire
Puffing with grey smoke.

We saw a trail of blood
Heading towards a rusty cage
And inside was a dead, slavery deer.

We didn't see goblins
On Goblin Mountain
But this was the closest we'd ever been
In our life.

Adam Clarke (10)
Red Rose Primary School, Chester-Le-Street

Spiders' Den

We didn't see spiders
In Spiders' Den
But we saw
Where the spiders had been.

We saw an antelope
That could only have been killed
By a deadly spider.

We saw poison puddles
That had fallen from killer fangs.

We saw knocked down trees.
We saw cracked boulders.

And draped from a branch
We saw a giant spider leg,
Hairy and bleeding.

We didn't see spiders
In Spiders' Den
But this was the closest
We'd ever been
To knowing.

Ryan Curry (9)
Red Rose Primary School, Chester-Le-Street

Mermaid Lagoon

We didn't see mermaids
In Mermaid Lagoon,
But we saw
Where the mermaids had been.

We saw fin marks in soft sand,
That were too big for any fish,
Only a mermaid could have made it.

We saw a handmade comb
Made from rocks from the seabed,
So beautiful no human could have made it.

We saw gorgeous glittering strands of hair
We saw silver stars in a beautifully carved box
A mermaid was carved on the lid.

We saw a pearl necklace,
So shiny, no human could have polished it
Mermaids, just mermaids could have done it.

We didn't see mermaids
In Mermaid Lagoon
But this was the closest
We'd ever been.

Lauren Wilson (10)
Red Rose Primary School, Chester-Le-Street

Mermaids Ocean

We didn't see mermaids
In Mermaid Ocean
But we saw
Where the mermaids had been.

We saw a colourful shell necklace,
That could only have been created
By a soft-handed mermaid.

We saw a very faint imprint of a mermaid's fin
That would only have been made
With a gentle tap on the sand.

We saw a shell bracelet,
We saw a bobble
Which had been worn by a mermaid.

And hung from a post, there was a locket
Which had been worn by a mermaid
And had a picture of her.

We didn't see mermaids
In Mermaids Ocean
But this was as close as
We'd ever get
To believing.

Caroline Ray (9)
Red Rose Primary School, Chester-Le-Street

Fairy Lake

We didn't see fairies
By the country lake
But we saw
Where the fairies had been.

We saw glistening shadows
That could have only been created
By the beautiful wings of a fairy.

We saw gold dust sprinkled on the ground
Where fairies had come to cry
And scattered their tears by the lake.

We saw miniature footprints
That only a tiny fairy could make
So careful and fair.

And by the lake there was a bright light
That could have only been a fairy's fiery eyes
Glowing . . . glowing . . . glowing.

We didn't see fairies
By the country lake
But this was the closest
We'd ever been
To knowing.

Emily Thompson (9)
Red Rose Primary School, Chester-Le-Street

Ogres' Wood

We didn't see ogres
In Ogres' Wood
But we saw
Where the ogres had been.

We saw big fat footprints
That could only have been made
By a big ogre.

We saw some puddles of water
Where we thought that the ogre
Had brought from the swamp.

We saw an old dusty book
Called 'How to be fierce'
We saw two skeletons.

And we found two
Big ogre shoes on
The floor.

We didn't see ogres
In Ogres' Wood
But we saw
Where the ogres had been
And we never stopped believing.

Elizabeth Ray (9)
Red Rose Primary School, Chester-Le-Street

My Holiday

At the start of the summer holidays
I went to Cyprus.
While I was there I got a girlfriend
Called Charlotte Gill.
But there was one part I did not like
Which was going to the beach because
The sand was too hot,
And the sea was very salty.
The bit I enjoyed the most was
Swimming in the pool,
Drinking cocktails and shandy,
And spending time with my
Girlfriend.

Kurt Dickinson (10)
Red Rose Primary School, Chester-Le-Street

Holiday To Italy

Once I went on holiday to Italy.
The hotel was nothing flash, but every morning
And night-time we could eat as much as we wanted.
Bolognese, pizza, steak, loads of different kinds of food,
I can still remember when my dad looked the other way
And I pinched his steak and ate it.
After, when we went to the hotel room
It was a fight between us and the naughty cockroaches.
My dad even flushed one down the toilet.
The next two weeks were a big adventure.
An aeroplane took me back to England at 3 o'clock in the morning.

Robert Jopling (10)
Red Rose Primary School, Chester-Le-Street

Fishing Holiday To America

Boxing Day was the day that we caught the plane to Boston.
There, we met Harry and went fishing for sharks,
I got a Hammerhead but my dad got it in!
Then we went for Bass.
I got two, my dad got five!
The next couple of days I got seven Stripey Bass.
I sold five to the fish shop.
The next day I got on the plane.
It took twelve hours to get back home
And that's my trip to America.

James Armstrong (10)
Red Rose Primary School, Chester-Le-Street

Into The Cauldron It Goes

Thrice the old miners' cats meowed,
Miners howl and children cry,
Ring the bell, 'tis time, 'tis time.

Round about the cauldron go,
In the mouldy cabbage throw,
Stone cold ginger hair, thick of lice,
Germ from Bilbo (sick from mice)
Boil up broccoli for the greenish smell,
Add sweaty cats, frog pie as well.

Stir it well, stir it good,
Stir it softly, stir it hard.

A fillet of an ancient snake,
In the cauldron boil and bake,
Eye of lizard and spawn of frog,
A heated log, a battered dog.

Stir it well, stir it good,
Stir it softly, stir it loud.

Joshua Allan (11)
St Pius X RC Primary School, Middlesbrough

Nana

Nana, why did you go?
Why did God have to lift you up on His golden wings?
And why was it you?

I am missing you Nana
Now more than ever
I wish we had more time, more time together.

God could have come back for you,
As stupid as it sounds
But I really miss you Nana,
I can't believe you've gone.

I feel like crying Nana,
Because life isn't the same anymore without you
But as long as I know we'll meet again
You will always stay in my heart.

Shanaz O'Brien (11)
St Pius X RC Primary School, Middlesbrough

Your Friend

Friends are people who kindly share,
Friends are people who really care.
They're not the people who push you to the ground,
Steal your pencils and boss you around.

Friends hug you and say you're great,
Give you gifts and call you mate.
They're not the people who call you Minnie,
Spotty, fat, scruffy or skinny.

Jus try to trust that one called mate,
Make sure they love you, friends don't *hate!*

Daisy Watkins (11)
St Pius X RC Primary School, Middlesbrough

Perfect Friend

Hands of Granddad
Feet of Gran
Throw them in our frying pan
Tongue of bat
Skin of snake
In the cauldron boil and bake
Legs of frog
Teeth of hog
Eye of owl
Hair of fowl.

Friend, friend perfect friend
One today I will send.

Alex McLoughlin (11)
St Pius X RC Primary School, Middlesbrough

Bombs Bash

Ladies die
Children cry
People clash
Bombs bash

Hearts sink
Little girl winks
Planes crash
Bombs bash

Hard day
No play
Legs clash
Bombs bash.

Louise Johnston (11)
St Pius X RC Primary School, Middlesbrough

My Pet

I have a dog called Bobby
He is black, he has
A very nice stack
Of toys, he jumps
Around and goes
Yap, yap, yap, he
Doesn't bite or
Frighten you, but he
Gets scared because
He is as big as
A felt-tip pen because
He is a Jack Russell
Puppy. He is very cute,
He likes to lick your
Face and hands.
That's my pet Bobby.

Victoria Young (9)
St Pius X RC Primary School, Middlesbrough

World War II

W orried children crying
O utside people dying
R ubble falling everywhere
L ittle ones cry for their lives
D iving bombs fall everywhere

W ar is a battle
A ll children evacuated
R ubble now killing people

T orn houses fall down
W ar is nearly over
O ver at last.

Faye Humphreys (11)
St Pius X RC Primary School, Middlesbrough

The Sun

I can shine bright
Without a light
And rise without
A switch.

I can make someone's
Day
Or look after your
Plants.

I can be a
Danger to your
Eyes,
And sometimes I
Can be too hot.

I can make a baby cry
From being me,
Or turn into rain
And be a pain.

Katie Vallely (10)
St Pius X RC Primary School, Middlesbrough

Winter

Winter is cold, your nose turns red.
Winter is a happy time, where children play.
Animals hibernate, waiting for spring.
Cars slide on the ice, struggling to stop.
Trees covered with fluffy white snow.
Detailed footprints on the ground by joyful children running wild.
Winter is the time when children have snow fights
When they come home wet, parents go mad
Winter is a happy time for everyone.

Jessica Connorton (11)
St Pius X RC Primary School, Middlesbrough

What's Rotten?

What's rotten? What's rotten?
Do I know?

Scabby toenails in a pot
Smelly boxers in a knot

The squashed frog with a toad
What a ploppy mode

Mirror, mirror on the wall
Is the farty master Paul?

Holey socks ready to pong
Nasty toenails growing too long

What's rotten? What's rotten?
Only one more thing

A green lump on the floor
The boy says I've got more

What's rotten? What's rotten?
I know it all!

Lewis Armes (11)
St Pius X RC Primary School, Middlesbrough

The Rain

I can seep through the soil with a great big whoosh
And drench the leaves with all my power.
I can spoil your day in everyway
And I'll flood a town with all my might.
I can soak you with my giant shower
And I'll give you my best shot of power.
I can calm myself down with a tiny little shower
And I'll leave you behind a nice slow breeze.

Charlotte Mett (9)
St Pius X RC Primary School, Middlesbrough

An Ordinary Day At School

When the teacher comes into class,
Everyone starts flicking grass.
Then the teacher says 'Stop, stop, stop!'
So that all the footballs go pop! Pop! Pop!

Now the bell has rung for break
All the dinner ladies start to bake.
Just then the bell rang for lunch,
So the teacher gives the blackboard a punch.

All the dinner's ready right now,
It's half a sheep and one full cow.
It is now the end of the day,
Everyone say
Hurray! Hurray!

Everyone likes it they're on their way home
But the mad teacher still ain't gone!

Daniel March (10)
St Pius X RC Primary School, Middlesbrough

My Family

My mum is great she can do eight times eight
She can do French and Spanish when she has no nail varnish.

But my dad has days in bed
When he lies in bed he's scratching his head
When he won't get up I tickle his feet.

And you know my brother who loves his mother
He hit me in the face but I didn't get a brace.

My nan is cool but she isn't a fool
She lets me sleep at her house where there isn't a mouse.

My grandad is sunny
And he knows the Easter bunny.

Ross McMenamin (10)
St Pius X RC Primary School, Middlesbrough

From Nightmares To Life!

Something is there
Although you can't see it
If you don't believe me
You'll never see it
If you say I'm joking
You better prepare, prepare
From a nightmare to life

If you eat cheese
But never say please
You better prepare
Before it gets there
Prepare, prepare
From a nightmare to life

There it is
Holding a dagger
The shadow of dread
Better not stagger
The lightning flashes
Run with the light
Run before the strike of twelve
The strike of midnight . . .

Michael Shaw (11)
St Pius X RC Primary School, Middlesbrough

The Sun

I shine on you
I do my job
I work all day just for you to have fun
If you upset me I will let the rain do her job
If you please me
I will shine until the end of the world.

Stephen Woodman (10)
St Pius X RC Primary School, Middlesbrough

A Day In School

Early on in the morning children wake,
When they see the morning sun they think
Today I'm going to bake.

Nine o'clock in the morning the bell goes for school,
The children moan and groan,
Wish there was a swimming pool.

Inside school working hard in maths,
Still wishing to go to the baths.

Half past ten, the bell goes,
Children zooming here and there,
Stripping their crisp packets bare.

Five to eleven the whistle goes,
Children line up in order
And start talking about Dr Forder.

Back inside to do more work
Some children just go berserk.

Twelve o'clock the bell goes
Children sometimes only eat a bean,
Some children even turn green.

Go inside to do our DT
My friend is here, he's with the BT.

Quarter past three, bling, bling goes the bell,
Children rejoice just as they zoom by Miss Boyce.

Jack Davies (10)
St Pius X RC Primary School, Middlesbrough

My Pet

My pet is the best you can get,
You can catch him with a net,
My pet is a flippy floppy fish.

Jack Bezance (9)
St Pius X RC Primary School, Middlesbrough

Animal Teachers Rock Or Rule

Reception's teacher's a monkey
Swinging up and down.
She roams all over
With a big crashing sound.

Year one's teacher's a monster,
A finger eater too
Just last week she escaped
From the zoo.

Year two's teacher's a rabbit,
Jumping up and down,
When you can hear her she'll
Be clapping all around.

Year three's teacher's
A little quiet mouse
But when she's talking
She'll collapse a house.

Year four's teacher's
A lion who never makes a sound,
But no one's stayed in the room
Not even for a pound.

Year five's teacher
A cheetah, a kangaroo too
Just two weeks
And it's off to Bandoo.

Year six's teacher
A dog from the sea,
But when she's around
She talks about me.

As for the head teacher
She's me!

Katie Wilson (10)
St Pius X RC Primary School, Middlesbrough

The Car

The car is bored most of the time
Sometimes it is a crime,
When it rains the car will get upset
And it will get wet, wet, wet.

Petrol is a cars favourite drink
But if you put too much in, it will sink,
The heat is one of a cars worse things
The windows break when someone sings.

It drives to long places
With lots of heavy cases,
When something hits the car,
It may get a bump or a scar.

When it gets very old
The car could get binned or sold,
When old people have a seat
Sometimes they need a reheat.

Nathan Newman (10)
St Pius X RC Primary School, Middlesbrough

My Mum And Dad

My mum's bingo crazy
And my dad's just lazy

My mum's sometimes hazy
While Dad's off with Daisy.

My mum comes in at eleven,
And dad feel likes he's in Heaven.

People say my dad's so funny
And people say my mum's a honey.

Aidan Chester (9)
St Pius X RC Primary School, Middlesbrough

Friends

Friends are there when you need them,
Friends are there when you don't,
Forget them! Surely I won't.

Friends are there to talk to,
Friends are there to play,
That's why we have fun every day.

Friends are there to help,
Friends are there to rely on,
That's how we know when they have gone.

Friends are there to trust,
Friends are there to love,
We know this because they are sent from God above.

Bethany James (9)
St Pius X RC Primary School, Middlesbrough

What Am I?

Seal teaser
Fish seizer
Ice lander
Storm stander
Egg cuddler
Warm huddler
Long waiter
Belly skater
Black back
White belly
Webbed feet
A comfy seat
What am I?

Chloe Welsh (10)
St Pius X RC Primary School, Middlesbrough

Lexuis

Lexuis is wild she acts like a young child.
From top to bottom night and day
Running around trying to play.
Tormenting my mum that's what she does
By ripping everything up and trailing muck.
For now my mum has no rest by picking up the things
That have been torn up in pieces.
By finding her dress and her high heels ripped up.
But after all she is only a pup
But some people class her as a little
Mutt!

Sarah Walker (10)
St Pius X RC Primary School, Middlesbrough

War

People lost their family and homes
Houses were smashed, no windows in sight
In the town they needed light
Children started to weep and cry
They saw their mothers and fathers die
The sirens beeped, they wouldn't go off
The fire and smoke made everyone cough
In the end when the war had ended
They wished their houses could be mended.

Louise Walker (11)
St Pius X RC Primary School, Middlesbrough

Batty

B ats are blind
A t the tiniest sound they hear, they disappear
T o a cave
T o hide away from
Y ou!

Connor Ovington (10)
St Pius X RC Primary School, Middlesbrough

My Mam

My mam she is the best,
She helps me with my homework.

Every day and every night I love my mam,
I help her and she helps me.
We'll be together forever.

My mam is the best mam anyone could ask for
She's my mam she is the best mam in the world.

I really, really, really love my mam.
My mam helps me that's why I really love her, my mam.

James Marsh (10)
St Pius X RC Primary School, Middlesbrough

Monday's Child

(Based on the nursery rhyme 'Monday's Child')

Monday's child stays in bed,
Tuesday's child likes to be fed,
Wednesday's child is lazy too,
Thursday's child needs to find a clue,
Friday's child screams and screams,
Saturday's child makes dreams and dreams,
But the child who is born on the Sabbath day
Is worse than ever, you know what the mothers say.

Chloe Jones (10)
St Pius X RC Primary School, Middlesbrough

Motorbikes

Motorbikes are blue
Some are green
Some are yellow
Motorbikes are good at pulling wheelies
Motorbikes are fast
Motorbikes.

Ryan Chilver (8)
St Pius X RC Primary School, Middlesbrough

Older Brother

Take one ounce of yelling mams,
Two ounces of football,
A sprinkle of chewing gum,
One screaming sister,
A bit of a really bad mister,
Get shoving, put in the oven,
Bake for sixty mins until cool and slick,
Rewind the shoving, take him out the oven,
Then you've got a brother
Who doesn't take after his mother,
But is really bad just like the dad.

Hayley Pink (9)
St Pius X RC Primary School, Middlesbrough

My Pet

My pet can't climb
My pet can't sing
My pet can't fly
My pet can't dance
My pet can't hide
My pet isn't small
My pet isn't tall
My pet is just a good dog.

Kyle McNamara (9)
St Pius X RC Primary School, Middlesbrough

Peanut Butter!

Peanut butter here and there
Peanut butter everywhere
I am thinking about eating some peanut butter
But I am having second thoughts
About using it on my brother!

Stephenie Roberts (8)
St Pius X RC Primary School, Middlesbrough

Weekend

Saturday we're off school,
Yes! Get to play out,
Get to play football,
Don't have to do any work,
Get to play out,
Get to see flowers,
Get to see everything,
Get
To
Play!

Jonathon Roche (8)
St Pius X RC Primary School, Middlesbrough

Dogs!

My dog is a Staff
Dogs make me laugh
Dogs make me cry
My dog popped my ball
My dog is lovely, he is so cuddly
My dog is so lovely, everyone thinks he's cuddly
My dog is called Rocky but I call him Rocksta
He is three years old.

Aaron Webber (9)
St Pius X RC Primary School, Middlesbrough

My Pet

My pet does not like water
My pet does not like barking
My pet does not like the dark
My pet does not like the sharks
My pet isn't slimy
My pet isn't that rough
My pet is a lovely, fluffy, cuddly *cat!*

Bradley Goulding (9)
St Pius X RC Primary School, Middlesbrough

Sunday

Sunday, Sunday what a day,
Don't have to get up for school today,
Sunday is a day of rest,
But I like playing with the rest,
Sunday, fun day all day long,
Please yourself or just have a rest,
But don't forget Sunday roast
And end the day with tea and toast.

Jessica Waite (8)
St Pius X RC Primary School, Middlesbrough

Lights

Bright lights
Of the thumping cold snow
Of the night
Bashing rain
On the windows
People walking home
In the dark night
Boys on the corner
Of the street talking.

Ellie Leopard (8)
St Pius X RC Primary School, Middlesbrough

My Pet

My pet isn't slimy
Slippery, sluggish, buggish
That's all the things it ain't

My pet is furry
With four legs
And two eyes
And it is a lovely hamster.

Andrew McElwee (9)
St Pius X RC Primary School, Middlesbrough

Mythical Monsters Beneath The Moat

Mythical monster beneath the moat
Mythical mermaids and leprechauns
Serpents in the well
Dragons in the dungeons
Fairies in the counting house
Pixies in the courtyard
Trolls beneath the mystical moat
Unicorns in the stable
With Pegasus in the sky.

Carl Alexander (8)
St Pius X RC Primary School, Middlesbrough

My TV

My TV does lots of things
When I turn it on it sings
I watch people sit and cry
And when a husband waves goodbye
I watch kids get in trouble
And babies in a bath blowing bubbles
I watch a robber rob a bank
I watch Titanic the boat that sank
These are what I watch on TV
I don't know about you but TV's for me!

Isabella Angioy (9)
St Pius X RC Primary School, Middlesbrough

Flame

Flame, flame
You dance about in the night
When I am not sleeping
Or when I am at school
I like you
And you like me.

Olivia Hopkin (8)
St Pius X RC Primary School, Middlesbrough

Bewitched

Walking through the corridor,
The creak of the stair.
I knew from that moment,
I knew she was there.

Whom am I talking about?
Who shall she be?
Why the lady in waiting,
Miss Courtney McGee.

The haunted sound,
The haunted scare.
The cackle of laughter,
Echoed in the air.

I turned around
And face to face.
A dreadful sight fell upon me,
My heart began to race.

Miss Courtney McGee,
Looked at me, her eyes open wide.
She said, 'Come with me!'
I went slow with every stride.

Until we came to a wooden door,
She looked at me once more.
She took me into a room
And went out and slammed the door.

I slammed at the bars
And screamed in pain,
I saw her fading away,
Would I ever see her again?

Sarah Dixon (10)
Shotton Hall Junior School, Peterlee

The Thing

It rolled over and swallowed everything,
It gulped it up,
It gulped it down,
It moved it forward,
Twisted it around.

Its colours swirled,
It tumbled,
It whirled.

The thing it was here,
Ever so near,
You will never believe me,
I know,
When I say that
The sea it
Rumbled and tumbled,
Turned, churned,
Gurgled, whirled
And suddenly
It changed.

It formed into gas, arose from its bed,
Fed up of resting its weary head,
It was off to travel the world instead,
It left my town and
Like I said, it
Rumbled and tumbled,
Turned, churned,
Gurgled and whirled,
With a flash of blinding light,
It was absorbed into the night.

Laura Weatherall (11)
Shotton Hall Junior School, Peterlee

Sunset Beautiful

Mam and Dad were asleep,
I was the only one awake,
I was on watch, I liked it.

The dolphins were swimming
Alongside the boat,
It was a lovely pleasurable time for me.

The sunset was a beautiful experience
Shining on the water -
Coming onto the boat,
It was a great odyssey.

It was a once-in-a-lifetime experience for me,
On the journey we stuck
Cheek by jowl together.

I've seen a flying fish, a basking shark,
They are very good creatures, I like them.

Adam Martin (11)
Shotton Hall Junior School, Peterlee

Once Upon A Time

Once upon a time
There was a rhyme
With two little kids so fine . . .

Hansel and Gretal, went down to settle
At the cottage of candy
To put on the kettle.
Then a witch came out
With a pink, fluffy snout
With glasses that looked almost metal
She was coming out, to give us a clout
But fell in a ditch
That'll fettle that witch!

Kirsty Fishwick (10)
Shotton Hall Junior School, Peterlee

Christmas Is Coming

Christmas is coming, it's nearly here
When stockings fill magically
It's the night before Christmas, it's very quiet
As I wait for the clock to chime midnight
I hear a sound like chimes
So I go downstairs to have a little peek, the bells are chiming
I rush back to bed, I fall straight to sleep
I wake the next morning
I check my phone, it's only five o'clock
So I sit and wait for another two hours
All of a sudden my door swings open
It is Mummy and Daddy
They think I'm asleep so I jump out on them
And give them a fright
We go downstairs to a big fright
Standing there was the puppy's might
I open my presents, I get a surprise
I got a new bike and some DVDs
My dog gets a bone and some little snacks.

Mark Gibson (11)
Shotton Hall Junior School, Peterlee

My School

My school does lots of art
The teachers are very smart
Maths, English, science too
These are all the things we do

Lots of interesting things to see
Why don't you just follow me
Around the school there are displays
Different achievements from sporting days.

Megan Thornley (8)
Shotton Hall Junior School, Peterlee

Friends

My friends mean the world to me,
Our friendship is just meant to be.
We go everywhere together
And we will be best friends forever.

Nothing will ever keep us apart,
They will always remain close to my heart.
We like to go shopping in the town
And they are always there when I'm feeling down.

A real friend is honest and true,
Who helps you out when you have the flu.
Good friends never fall out
Or ever scream and shout.

My friends mean the world to me,
Our friendship is just meant to be.
We go everywhere together
And we will be best friends forever.

Kirsty Anne Farn (10)
Shotton Hall Junior School, Peterlee

Christmas And New Year

On Christmas Day,
I love to play,
With all my games and toys.
I got some books
And lots of stuff
And that was enough.
On New Year's Day,
I love to play
With party poppers and games.
I got a pound
And heard a sound,
The bells were ringing!
Happy New Year!

Michael Newhouse (11)
Shotton Hall Junior School, Peterlee

Once Upon A Rhyme

Once upon a rhyme
So far back in time
I woke up in my bed
I had a really bad head

I went outside to explore
I couldn't see anything more
I saw Robin Hood
As clearly as I could

I saw the gingerbread man
He was thinking of a plan
To stop the fox from eating him
He had some help from little Tim

Aladdin was flying his carpet
While I was going to market
I saw Rapunzel let down her hair
I don't know how she gets it so fair

I saw the three bears
But really no one cares
I saw the three little pigs
They were playing with twigs.

Liam Goodfellow (9)
Shotton Hall Junior School, Peterlee

Blue Is . . .

The calm blue sea on a summer's day
The fine raindrops
Falling to Earth
The colour of ice-cold water
The colour of a parrot's tail
The colour of a streaking ribbon
The colour of winter ice.

Nicholas Turnbull (10)
Shotton Hall Junior School, Peterlee

Life On The Boat

The sun is rising,
I am waiting by myself,
I can hear everything and the sea
And the birds are quite excited.

I can hear Dad snoring,
Stella is on her back and she is running,
Mam is sound asleep.

On the boat Mam was the skipper,
Dad is the shipmate,
Stella was the ship's cat
And I am the ship's boy.

Mam and Dad are always
Having games of chess - I don't,
I play with Stella Artois all the time.

Now I have seen Africa, I can tell everyone.

Joanne Holborg (10)
Shotton Hall Junior School, Peterlee

Once Upon A Rhyme

Once upon a rhyme
I went back in time
I saw beautiful Snow White
It was late in the night
And I gave her a fright

Once upon a rhyme
I went back in time
I saw Little John and Robin Hood
Firing arrows through the wood

Once upon a rhyme
I went back in time
I saw a small hand
It was Alice in Wonderland!

Alex Gibson (10)
Shotton Hall Junior School, Peterlee

Red Is . . .

Red reminds you of danger!
A shy face or rosy cheeks,
The flame burning behind an angry man,
The nerves ticking because you're scared.

Red reminds you to *stop!*
The flash goes through you of the traffic lights,
The blood on a knife in an attack,
The glint of anger,
A ruby.

Samantha Hepworth (11)
Shotton Hall Junior School, Peterlee

The Glitter Lamp

Like a moon shining ever so bright,
With stars around it brightening the night,
Like a splash of a puddle frozen in mid-air,
Like a clown's fuzzy hair flopping happily,
Like a chimney sweep's brush, covered in dust,
Like a bird flying in the gentle breeze,
Like a warm fire on a winter's night.

Lauren Bannister (10)
Shotton Hall Junior School, Peterlee

The Glitter Lamp

Like a firework bursting with sparkling lights,
Like a moon's glitter at night,
Like a waterfall gushing with blue,
Like a peacock's tail swaying in the green fields,
Like a bird's wings flying in the summer skies,
Like a feather glowing in the midnight sky.

Tasmin Duggan (11)
Shotton Hall Junior School, Peterlee

Michael - My Thoughts

I am sitting here on watch tonight,
You really should see the beautiful sight,
It's calm and cool here sitting in the cockpit,
It's lovely just being able to sit,
I'm usually working hard all day,
Just every now and then I get to play,
The flying fish are here with me,
So really they're my company,
This sunset is so beautiful and colourful,
I saw, the other day, a great big gull,
I've been to Azores, we stopped for two nights,
My mum and dad had the smallest fight,
I hope I see my friends and family again,
Then they will begin to be more of a pain,
I enjoyed my odyssey!

Sarah French (10)
Shotton Hall Junior School, Peterlee

My First Day

School holidays are at an end
And I'm going round the bend
My shoes are on the wrong way
I shout - 'I'm not going!'

But I get to the gates
And play with my mates
Then when we all go in
We put our rubbish in the bin

We get to the stairs
And the teacher just stares - *at me!*
Going back to school
Oh no!

Tim Evans (11)
Shotton Hall Junior School, Peterlee

Ingredients Of Friendship

F riends are people who play together,
R espect each other in every way.
I f any of us fall apart,
E very time we'll go back to the start.
N ever, ever laugh behind backs,
D ecide together,
S o go on, be a friend,
H elp each other,
I n every way,
P lease be a friend, just be a friend.

Annie Harris (9)
Shotton Hall Junior School, Peterlee

Friends

F is for friendship which can't be lost
R is for relationship which is so special
I is for invite your friend around
E is for everlasting friendship
N is for being nice to ensure a good friendship
D is for denial which should never happen
S is for safety with your friends.

Vicky Bentham (10)
Shotton Hall Junior School, Peterlee

Bluey

I am a dolphin
My name is Bluey
I like to swim with my friend Louie
I am five, he is three
And he can swim faster than me
We always have fish for tea
My friend Louie and me.

Michelle Burey (11)
Shotton Hall Junior School, Peterlee

Friendship

F riends are real
R espect is glorious
I gnorance will get you nowhere
E verybody would like a special friend
N otice that if you are cruel you will never have friends
D on't ever be nasty to friends
S ensational, happiness is the best
H onesty is what a friend needs
I f you have good friends, be kind to them
P lease, please, please be a friend.

Paige McGoldrick (9)
Shotton Hall Junior School, Peterlee

Sam And Ben

Sam's my little brother
He really is a pest
But as far as little brothers go
He really is the best

Ben's my other brother
We are a group of three
But the best thing about being eldest
Is the fact the boss is *me!*

Jack Anderson (9)
Shotton Hall Junior School, Peterlee

A Snake

The snake softly slides
Through the green trees
It hisses through the night
Softly, silently
Then darts for its prey!

Victoria Dennis (8)
Skerne Park Primary School, Darlington

The School Day

It's 8 o'clock
Get ready for school,
Pick a top
Which one looks cool?

No uniform
Just for the day,
I think it's great
What do you say?

Catch the bus
Grab a seat,
He's stepped in dog muck
Just look at his feet!

The first class
Start of school
I've forgotten my homework
I'm such a fool!

Even more classes
Science and history
English and French
Maths and RE

I'm going home
No clubs today,
School is quite cool
What do you say?

Terri Stephens (11)
Skerne Park Primary School, Darlington

The Girl Called Crystal

There was a girl called Crystal
Who had a water pistol
She squirted water everywhere
Even at a grizzly bear.

Shivaun Barnes (10)
Skerne Park Primary School, Darlington

Alone

My friends are not very kind,
I'm going beetroot-red,
My mind is going mad with me,
Things flying round in my head.

I don't like it,
I feel like I'm going to cry,
They're meant to be my friends,
I can't even say goodbye.

They're walking away from me,
As though they don't like me now,
But I know they did before,
They never used to start a row.

I can see them staring at me,
Watching me go by,
They think I don't know,
But they're only telling me a lie.

Ashley Pascoe (11)
Skerne Park Primary School, Darlington

Snow Pony

Little pony, pretty pony
Smallest in the herd
Rearing, frightened
Timid as a bird
You canter away
Kicking the snow
I watch you race
Neighing as you go
Little pony, pretty pony
So precious to me
You're a little snow pony
And you're wild
And you're free.

Lily McGonigal (8)
Skerne Park Primary School, Darlington

The Abandoned Puppy

One day I was in the yard,
When I heard a little tap,
There stood a box made out of card,
So I opened the little flap.

There was a puppy as miserable as could be,
I looked at it and had to take it home,
So I walked with the puppy whining for its mummy,
Soon as I got home I gave the dog a bone.

I started to pick names,
But they were all wrong,
Picking names was a bit of a game,
I turned around one day to find the puppy was gone.

I shouted 'Love' upon the streets,
That was the puppy's new name,
There was my puppy by the park seat,
She thought it was a game.

Then I turned round to see a blind old man sitting there,
I gave him Love as his guide dog and he grinned.

So if you ever see an abandoned puppy or any other animal at all,
Please phone the RSPCA for help.

Annabel Townsend (11)
Skerne Park Primary School, Darlington

Twinkle

There I stand, making pictures in the sky,
Watching the moon drift away,
I feel as if I'm in a dream,
Not wanting to go to bed,
Knowing it is time to sleep,
I lay staring up above,
Lying down, I float away into a dream,
Even though I'm in a dream,
I feel as if I'm wide awake.

Lauren Mitchinson (11)
Skerne Park Primary School, Darlington

My Friend

My friend is nice
Nice as a day
He plays with me
All the time
He is good
As good as a dream team
He is the best at football in our class
He is as good as Van Nistelrooy
He is good
Mint
He is the best out of Lee
He is famous
He has some fans
And skins all the football
He's scored twenty goals in two days.

Jordan Bateman (8)
Skerne Park Primary School, Darlington

Litter

I'm unhappy
about
litter
being
dropped
on the
floor when
there is
a bin
a
b
o
u
t.

Stacy Knight (8)
Skerne Park Primary School, Darlington

My Teacher

Whistle blower
Child watcher
Kid learner
Story reader
Work helper
Primetime chooser
Maths learner
Hand writer
Computer worker
Work checker
Register marker.

Kayleigh Reddington (8)
Skerne Park Primary School, Darlington

Free Spirit

H ow fast are they as they fly through the air?
O ver the jumps, gracefully clearing the pole,
R unning and galloping along the beach,
S ometimes racing waves, never stopping,
E very day roaming free, lucky creature,
S o happy in a herd, they're never alone and never will be.

Caitlin Longstaff (11)
Skerne Park Primary School, Darlington

My Kitten

My kitten is a newborn
My kitten plays with a horn
My kitten rolls on the lawn
My kitten chews up Dad's uniform
My kitten decided to get my picture torn
My kitten likes being newborn
He gets away with *everything!*

Luci Purves (8)
Skerne Park Primary School, Darlington

My New Sister

She is going to be beautiful,
She is going to be good
And clever
And shiny.
She's going to have a skirt
And loads of dresses,
She's going to be small
And she's going to get all the boys
And I'm going to look after her.

Andrew Colley (8)
Skerne Park Primary School, Darlington

Our Caretaker

Mr Elliot is small and round,
We always see him walking around.
He wears a hat and blue overalls,
He always gets the balls off the roof
And kicks them back with a hoof.
Our caretaker is Mr Elliot,
We think he is really brilliant.

Paige Cooper (9)
Skerne Park Primary School, Darlington

Magic Power

The tap of a wand,
the zoom of a broomstick,
the laugh of a witch,
the hoot of an owl,
the cloak of an enchanted wizard,
the shooting star flying round the Earth,
the rubies, sapphires, the diamonds,
join force to make *magic power!*

Elijah Taylor (10)
Skerne Park Primary School, Darlington

Locked In

Trapped, no one to talk to,
Alone, when your friends are out on the street,
I'm stuck in my room with nothing to do.

Not allowed to watch the TV or listen to music,
Empty inside, all I can do is sleep,
Till my parents tell me I'm allowed out.

Despaired and angry,
To be out,
But, still locked out!

Zoe Hunter (11)
Skerne Park Primary School, Darlington

My Grandad

Funny and happy
Loving and warm
Starring role
Wonderful man
Heart of gold
Kind and helpful
That's my grandad!

Victoria Butcher (11)
Skerne Park Primary School, Darlington

Locked In

Stuck inside a classroom,
Nowhere to go,
The teachers shouting
Like they have never done before,
We do some work, which is very depressing,
What could I do with freedom?

Christopher House (11)
Skerne Park Primary School, Darlington

All About My Mum

My mum respects me
My mum loves me to bits
My mum is the best
My mum is my best friend
My mum is a really nice person to meet
My mum has bought me a dog called Mitzi
And she has had eight puppies
When I go and see my mum she is always pleased to see me
And she has always got something for me
My mum is the best in the world
And that is why I love her so!

Amanda Fitzpatrick (10)
Skerne Park Primary School, Darlington

My Teacher

My teacher is a good colourer,
He isn't bad at all
And he never needs the toilet through the lesson.
He's a good teacher
And a good piano person.
He can sing like God,
He lets me take the register,
He's a good friend
And he always solves problems,
He always gets on with me.

Ryan Burton (8)
Skerne Park Primary School, Darlington

Dad

D rives his car to work
A nd he drives it back again
D id his job all day long and went back to bed again.

Christopher Hull (10)
Skerne Park Primary School, Darlington

My Auntie

Heart of silver
Dog lover
Stall worker
Flower maker
Children carer
Cat hater
Kind and helpful
Loving and warm
Really kind
Wonderful woman
Kind hearted
The best auntie in the world
That's my auntie.

Autumn Robson (11)
Skerne Park Primary School, Darlington

Balloons

Balloons, balloons,
In the sky,
Popping away,
Helium spray.

Floating upwards,
Through the air,
As the sun shines,
A reflection glares.

While it moves,
Through the clouds,
I watch it go, go, go,
As it . . .

Rebecca Stirland (11)
Skerne Park Primary School, Darlington

Mam And Dad

M y mam works at Primark
A nd my mam looks after my friends
M y mam is neat

A nd sometimes mad
N ow when I am at home she can be kind
D own at the floor working

D rives a car
A nd sometimes is kind
D rives me down to the park.

Sarah Dunn (9)
Skerne Park Primary School, Darlington

Best Friend!

F riend, friend in the park,
R achel, are you going to school?
I ce cream we like!
E ven at home I talk to her
N ever ever break up
D on't break *in!*

Rachel Curle (10)
Skerne Park Primary School, Darlington

Deceitfulness

I have a crocodile in me
It is sly and cunning
It eats and eats
It is fast and slow
It has a big mouth and sharp teeth
It prances and kills
It's not lazy and works hard
It scares its intruders
And never gives up!

David Bigham (8)
Viewley Hill Primary School, Middlesbrough

Young Writers - Once Upon A Rhyme Northern Counties

What Happens To Gabrielle Plants?

Gabrielle loved eating plants
She even stuffed them down her pants
And when she went to France
Her mother found her eating them with fleshy ants
When the next day came, she awoke with a terrible fright
That her body had turned into a plant in the middle of the night
Her mother wondered why she had turned green
Because it was the greenest green she had ever seen
Finally one day her mother told her, 'Don't eat them'
As she grew an enormous stem
Then it came to a terrible day
She turned yellow and slipped away . . .

Gabrielle Leighton (8)
Viewley Hill Primary School, Middlesbrough

Running Rabbit

I have a rabbit in me,
It digs in the ground,
It tickles inside me,
It scratches me with its sharp claws,
It eats carrots with its two front teeth,
It has a little white tail,
It can pounce like a kangaroo.

Kierra Sargent (8)
Viewley Hill Primary School, Middlesbrough

Relaxed

I have a bear in me,
It is soft and warm,
It is cuddly,
It cuddles with its cubs,
It is full of energy,
It runs round the mountain with its cubs.

Bradley Wilkinson (8)
Viewley Hill Primary School, Middlesbrough

Ellie Smelly

There once was a girl called Ellie Smelly,
She always ate lots of jelly,
Her mum did not know what to do,
So she went to the zoo,
She looked for a wobbly treat,
But all she found were smelly feet,
So she said, 'Ellie, if you lose your feet,
You could get these feet full of meat.'
So one day somehow she lost her feet,
So she got the meat to put on her feet,
The next day when she was walking down the street,
A dog came along and bit her feet,
So she crawled to the dump,
To get some meat and found a great big lump,
What she found was toxic jelly
And that was the end of Ellie Smelly!

Lewis Danks (9)
Viewley Hill Primary School, Middlesbrough

Master Curly Wig

There was a man called Mr Curly Wig,
Who just loved to eat some figs,
One day his curls began to glow
And his ears turned into snow,
His curls they grew and grew and grew
And then he got the terrible flu,
His curls began to grow so big,
He even began to stop eating figs,
He thought he'd get his curls took
And turned out to have a brand new look,
His curls grew inside his belly,
He began to feel really smelly,
One day he went to the shop,
Then through the doorway he went *pop!*

Ashley Charlton (9)
Viewley Hill Primary School, Middlesbrough

Jim-Bob Boo Who Was Scared Of The Loo

Jim-Bob Boo was scared of the loo
Sadly his mum did not know what to do
She tried to put him on the pot
But he began to cry a lot

She tried to bribe him with some sweets
But he said, 'I'd rather do it in the street!'
So he ran outside to do his thing
Until he heard the doorbell ring . . .

So he toddled to his home to see who it was
'Why are you here?' he said,
'Because . . . I am the ancient prickly tree
I really don't like it when you wee!

I'm going to throw you into the highest tree,
To make you think when you wee!'
He stayed there in sun and wind and rain
And he was never seen again!

Mikki-Jo Blades (9)
Viewley Hill Primary School, Middlesbrough

Scary Poem

Mr Scary was so hairy
Until one day he turned into a fairy
He phoned the doctor, called Mr Procter
He said, 'There's no cure for this
But you might live longer if you eat fish'
'But fish is horrible,' said Mr Scary
'It may make you less hairy'
'Don't be a fool
I'd rather have a swimming pool
I love my hairs, they're better than pears
I'll die if I have to
I'll only be scared of the loo'
The next day came
He died walking down the lane.

Matthew Kay (9)
Viewley Hill Primary School, Middlesbrough

Before The Inspection . . .

Rays of sun heat me
Sharpened pencil do not snap on me
Chair stay on six legs for me
Dictionary do not rip on me

As my pencil writes on the page
Do not squiggle on me
As the inspector looks at my work
Keep my fear to myself

Smart computer do not crash on me
Display do not fall on me
Tray stay tidy for me
Lead me to the inspection . . .

Ryan Phillips (9)
Viewley Hill Primary School, Middlesbrough

Laziness!

I have a tortoise inside me,
It slowly walks across me,
Its laziness takes over inside me,
Its loneliness hurts me,
It tries to run in me.

Katie Taylor (8)
Viewley Hill Primary School, Middlesbrough

Happiness

I have a dolphin in me
It feels calm
It giggles when people clap
It holds the knowledge of a thousand men
It feels happy when it dives
It feels exciting when I swim.

John-Paul Stone (9)
Viewley Hill Primary School, Middlesbrough

The Jolly Dolphin

I have a dolphin in me,
It jumps and swims all day,
It swims and squawks,
It is a cute dolphin,
It goes to sleep,
It eats loads of fish,
It jumps up really mad,
It likes the colour of blue.

Rachael Miller (9)
Viewley Hill Primary School, Middlesbrough

Can't Make My Mind Up

I have a bear in me
Warm and cuddly
And calm and sleepy
It could erupt at any time
It makes me nervous
It pulls down trees with strong paws
All full of anger and strength.

Billy Horrigan (9)
Viewley Hill Primary School, Middlesbrough

I Have A Wolf In Me

I have a wolf in me
It roars very loud
It slavers like ice cream drips
It lays calm and still
It sometimes scratches me
It sometimes tickles me
But still I love it inside of me!

Samantha Lappin (9)
Viewley Hill Primary School, Middlesbrough

Sneakiness

I have a snake in me
It tickles and wriggles
It is slimy and sticky
It is sneaky and slithers
It slithers up trees
It hides in trees
It gets caught in nets
People want to kill it.

Jay Morrison (9)
Viewley Hill Primary School, Middlesbrough

I Have A Monkey In Me!

I feel cheeky
I feel jumpy
I feel joyful
I feel happy
I feel full of freedom
I feel kind
I feel funny.

Amber Daly (9)
Viewley Hill Primary School, Middlesbrough

Mr Kerr

He's an inflatable chair
He's an energetic monkey
Swinging from tree to tree
He's a sunny spring day with occasional showers
The smell of a wild forest
The colour bright orange
The sound of a splashing, crashing waterfall
A spicy chicken massala with a fizzy drink.

Anthony Kippax (10)
Village Primary School, Thornaby

Town Centre

The shoppers are like athletes running for the finish line,
The bright lights are like luminous stars twinkling on a
                                        black panther's paw,
The office blocks are like a mob of mams in the playground,
The bus is like an enormous lawnmower picking up long green grass,
The car parks are like a pack of mad football supporters
Jumping up and down from a tremendous goal,
The shops are like a sold out wrestling event.

Arron Butta (11)
Village Primary School, Thornaby

The Busy Town

The shoppers are like a stampede of elephants
The bright lights are like bright, sparkling stars
The office blocks are like spaceships with mysterious gadgets inside
The bus is like a ship sailing across the sea
The car parks are like crowded trees in a sombre forest
The shops are like busy mazes.

Vanessa Butterworth (11)
Village Primary School, Thornaby

Happiness

The touch of a gentle butterfly
The smell of sweet strawberries
And the sight of the sunset setting
With the sound of the church bells ringing
The taste of luxurious white wine.

Daniel Thompson (11)
Village Primary School, Thornaby

Miss Rout

She's a bouncy chair
She's a pouncing puppy
A happy deer
She's a sunny day with a drop of rain
The smell of roses blooming in the spring
The colour baby-blue
The sound of a screeching bird
She's a cherry bakewell.

Jodie Richardson (10)
Village Primary School, Thornaby

Grandad

Grandad was as old as the grassy meadows
Hair like dandelion clocks
I remember that to the end
Like a bracken fire on a hillside
He puffed out great clouds of smoke
Motionless like a grassy mound
He sat in his favourite chair.

Lauren Atkinson (9)
Village Primary School, Thornaby

My Friend, Emma

Emma is as white as the winter snow, cool and delicate
She tastes of white wine, chilled and still
She smells of relaxing lavender
And sounds like the joy on Christmas Day
She is warm and cuddly and soft.

Toby Beech (11)
Village Primary School, Thornaby

Mr Christine

He's an old wooden rocking chair
He's a gentle giraffe
He's a windy evening in autumn
The smell of strong coffee
The colour mossy-green
The sound of a breeze blowing through the trees -
Sometimes gentle, sometimes howling
He's a traditional Sunday dinner with a glass of beer.

Leigh Riley (11)
Village Primary School, Thornaby

My Friend Elizabeth

Elizabeth is as green as a leaf on a flower
She tastes of sweet Granny Smith's apples
She smells of chocolate being melted in a glass bowl
And sounds like joy being spread in the world
She feels soft as a pillow on a bed.

Emily Tatters (10)
Village Primary School, Thornaby

My Friend Karina

Karina is calm like the colour blue,
She is cheesy like a marguerita pizza,
She smells like refreshing nature
And is loud like a gushing waterfall,
She is valuable like a hard, expensive, modern sofa.

Amy Oram (11)
Village Primary School, Thornaby

The River

The river is a brute tiger,
Wild and free,
Violently he roams and destroys
Everything in his path,
Hour after hour he ferociously tears
Up the plants and trees,
Roaring! Roaring! Roaring!
He bursts to the sea.

But on quiet days of May and June,
As the sun beats down on the grassy banks
He barely moves,
Peacefully he runs over the rocky landscape,
So sleek, so sleek,
Purring as the night draws on.

Hannah-Marie Healey (10)
Village Primary School, Thornaby

The River

The river is a slithering snake meandering and peaceful
He trickles past the muddy banks
With relaxed jaws and long extended body
Hour upon hour he eats away the boggy banks
The giant snake eats, eats, eats, gulping down his food.

Catherine Pillar (10)
Village Primary School, Thornaby

Happiness

Happiness is as yellow as a banana
It tastes like citrus fruits
It smells of expensive, luxurious Belgian chocolate
It sounds like a bird chirping in summer
It feels like a gooey sweet.

David Campbell (11)
Village Primary School, Thornaby

The Town Centre

The shoppers are like crazy dogs hunting for food
The bright lights are like sparkling crystal balls
The office blocks are like huge cardboard boxes
The bus is like a long, loud party
The car parks are like enormous black tiles
The shops are like mad classrooms in schools.

Karina LeFevre (10)
Village Primary School, Thornaby

My Friend Jodie

Jodie is as blue as the calm sea
She tastes like a sweet and sour lemon
She smells like a hot dog sizzling in the pan
And sounds like a trumpet in an orchestra
She feels like a warm and soft teddy.

Elizabeth Foster (10)
Village Primary School, Thornaby

Anger

Anger is red, raging and wrath
It tastes of a chilli, spicy and hot
It smells of thorny bushes
And sounds like a diabolical, roaring lion
It feels like a hedgehog, thorny and prickly.

Thomas Chilton (11)
Village Primary School, Thornaby

Seeing Grandma

Stumbling, she hobbles
With knobbly knees
Shaking like a scared animal
Wobbling

She squashes your body
Nearly, with gnarled
Twisting, ancient hands

She makes you sit, tied
She then crams you full
With Sunday dinner and Coke

She glares while you eat
Her fabulous food
She milks you dry of answers
About the present she gave you.

Emma Burridge (11)
Village Primary School, Thornaby

The Town Centre

The shoppers are like a stampede
Shoving around the shops.
The bright lights are like enormous eyes
Watching people go by.
The office blocks are like huge tins
With people inside.
The buses are like snakes
Slithering between buildings.
The car parks are like chalkboards
With chalk lines drawn on them.
The shops are like cubes in the middle
Of the town centre.

Sophie Fishburn (10)
Village Primary School, Thornaby